POCKET CHEF

Pies

igloobooks

igloobooks

Published in 2016
by Igloo Books Ltd
Cottage Farm
Sywell
NN6 0BJ
www.igloobooks.com

Food photography and recipe development:
© Stockfood, The Food Media Agency
Cover image © Stockfood, The Food Media Agency

LEO002 0816
2 4 6 8 10 9 7 5 3
ISBN: 978-1-78557-541-9

Cover designed by Nicholas Gage
Interiors designed by Charles Wood-Penn
Edited by Natalie Baker

Printed and manufactured in China

Contents

Pastry

PASTRY

Shortcrust Pastry

MAKES 350 G / 12 OZ

PREPARATION TIME 5 MINUTES

COOKING TIME 40 MINUTES

INGREDIENTS

250 g / 9 oz / 1 ⅔ cups plain (all-purpose) flour,
    plus extra for dusting
a pinch of salt
125 g / 4 ½ oz / ½ cup unsalted butter,
    cold and cubed
55 ml / 2 fl. oz / ¼ cup ice cold water

METHOD

1. Sift the flour and salt into a food processor.
   Add the butter and pulse until it resembles
   fine breadcrumbs.

2. Add half of the water and pulse again until a
   dough starts to come together. Add a little
   more water if the dough is too dry, pulsing
   briefly between additions.

3. Turn out the dough onto a lightly floured
   surface and knead gently for 30 seconds
   until even.

4. Flatten the dough and wrap in cling film,
   then chill for at least 30 minutes.

5. Turn out the dough and roll out on a lightly
   floured surface before using.

Flaky Pastry

MAKES 650 G / 1 LB 7 OZ

PREPARATION TIME 5 MINUTES

COOKING TIME 1 HOURS 10–15 MINUTES

INGREDIENTS

250 g / 9 oz / 1 ⅔ cups strong plain (all-purpose)
  flour, plus extra for dusting
1 tsp salt
250 g / 9 oz / 1 cup unsalted butter,
  at room temperature
125–175 ml / 4 ½–6 fl. oz / ½–¾ cup iced water

METHOD

1. Sift the flour and salt into a mixing bowl.
   Break chunks of butter into the flour and
   incorporate with your fingertips until it
   resembles rough breadcrumbs.

2. Add two-thirds of the water and start to mix
   until a dough forms.

3. Cover the dough with cling film and chill for
   30 minutes. Once rested, knead and roll into
   a 20 cm x 50 cm (8 in x 20 in) rectangle on a
   lightly floured surface.

4. Fold the top down to the middle and bring
   the bottom end back over the fold on top.
   Turn the dough 90 degrees and roll out into a
   20 cm x 50 cm (8 in x 20 in) rectangle as
   above, then repeat the folding step.

5. Wrap the pastry in greaseproof paper and
   chill for 30 minutes.

PASTRY

Hot Water Pastry

MAKES 450 G / 1 LB

PREPARATION TIME 5 MINUTES

COOKING TIME 1 HOUR 40 MINUTES

INGREDIENTS

250 g / 9 oz / 1 ²/₃ cups plain (all-purpose) flour,
    plus extra for dusting
110 ml / 4 fl. oz / ½ cup water
55 g / 2 oz / ¼ cup unsalted butter
3 tbsp lard
½ tsp salt

METHOD

1. Sift the flour into a bowl and set to one side.
   Combine the water, butter, lard and salt in a
   saucepan, cooking over a medium heat until
   the fats have melted.

2. Pour into the flour and mix with a wooden
   spoon until a rough dough forms, then cover
   with a tea towel and leave to rest at room
   temperature for 1 hour.

3. After resting, turn out the dough onto a
   floured surface and gently knead and fold
   the dough for 2–3 minutes until even
   and soft.

4. Cover and chill for 30 minutes before
   turning out and using.

'uff Pastry

AKES 450 G / 1 LB

EPARATION TIME 5–10 MINUTES

OKING TIME 45–50 MINUTES

GREDIENTS

5 g / 8 oz / 1 ½ cups strong white plain flour,
 plus extra for dusting
inch of salt
5 g / 8 oz / 1 cup unsalted butter,
 cold and cubed
0 ml / 4 fl. oz / ½ cup iced water
sp lemon juice

METHOD

1. Sift the flour and salt into a large mixing bowl.

2. Add a quarter of the butter and rub into the
   flour until soft, then gradually add the water
   and the lemon juice, mixing until a soft,
   elastic dough forms.

3. Roll out the dough on a floured surface into
   a rectangle three times as long as it is wide;
   it should be approximately 1 cm (½ in) thick.

4. Arrange a quarter of the diced butter across
   the top two-thirds of the dough. Fold the
   bottom third up and the top third down, turn
   90 degrees to the right and seal the edges.

5. Repeat this step until all the butter has been
   used up, turning the pastry 90 degrees
   each time.

6. Cover and chill before using.

PASTRY

Suet Pastry

MAKES 450 G / 1 LB

PREPARATION TIME 5 MINUTES

COOKING TIME 5–10 MINUTES

INGREDIENTS

300 g / 10 ½ oz / 2 cups self-raising flour
a pinch of salt
150 g / 5 oz / ⅔ cup shredded beef suet
55 ml / 2 fl. oz / ½ cup iced water

METHOD

1. Sift the flour and salt into a large mixing bowl
2. Add the suet and stir well to mix, then start
   to add the water, 1 tbsp at a time. Mix with a
   knife until the mixture starts to come
   together as a dough.
3. If the dough is too dry, add a little more
   water and continue to mix until it
   clumps together.
4. Mix the dough with your hands, until smooth
   and elastic, then use.

Choux Pastry

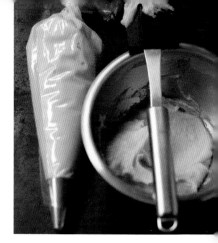

MAKES 450 G / 1 LB

PREPARATION TIME 5 MINUTES

COOKING TIME 10 MINUTES

INGREDIENTS

150 g / 5 oz / ⅔ cup butter, cubed
300 ml / 10 ½ fl. oz / 1 ¼ cups semi-skimmed milk
1 tsp salt or 1 tsp caster (superfine) sugar
150 g / 5 oz / 1 cup plain (all-purpose) flour, sifted
4 large eggs

METHOD

1. Combine the butter, milk and salt or sugar in a saucepan. Warm over a medium heat, stirring occasionally, until the butter has melted and the liquid is simmering.

2. Remove from the heat and beat in the flour, stirring constantly, until the dough leaves the sides of the pan.

3. Return the saucepan to a medium heat and cook, stirring frequently, for 2 minutes before beating in the eggs, one by one. The pastry should be glossy and of dropping consistency.

4. Spoon the pastry into a piping bag fitted with a nozzle before using.

Meat Pies

Meat and Potato Pie

SERVES 6

PREPARATION TIME 20 MINUTES

COOKING TIME 1 HOUR 10–20 MINUTES

INGREDIENTS

2 tbsp sunflower oil
1 large onion, chopped
2 rashers of bacon, chopped
2 small carrots, peeled and sliced
2 large floury potatoes, peeled and diced
600 g / 1 lb / 4 cups beef mince
a dash of Worcestershire sauce
500 ml / 18 fl. oz / 2 cups beef stock
450 g / 1 lb prepared flaky pastry
a little plain (all-purpose) flour, for dusting
1 large egg, beaten

METHOD

1. Preheat the oven to 180°C (160°C fan) / 35[?] / gas 4.

2. Heat the oil in a large casserole dish set over a medium heat until hot, then add the onion, bacon, carrot and potato and sweat for 8–10 minutes until softened.

3. Add the beef mince and stir well, cooking until browned all over, then add the Worcestershire sauce and cover with the stock.

4. Bring to a simmer, then cook over a reduce[d] heat for 15 minutes, stirring occasionally.

5. Take two-thirds of the pastry and roll out o[n] a floured surface into a round approximate[ly] 1 cm (½ in) thick.

6. Use the round of pastry to line the base an[d] sides of a 20 cm (8 in) pie dish that has bee[n] lined with greaseproof paper. Prick the bas[e] with a fork before chilling.

7. Roll out the remaining pastry into a 22 cm (9 in) round approximately 1 cm (½ in) thick[.] Fill the pastry case with the beef filling, the[n] lift the pastry lid on top and seal against the edge.

8. Crimp the rim with the tines of a fork, then brush the top with beaten egg and cut out a small hole in the centre. Bake for 40–50 minutes until the pastry is cooked and golden.

Meat and Vegetable Pie

SERVES 4

PREPARATION TIME 15 MINUTES

COOKING TIME 1 HOUR 35–45 MINUTES

INGREDIENTS

750 g / 1 lb 10 oz / 5 cups chuck steak,
   trimmed and cubed

2 tbsp plain (all-purpose) flour,
   plus extra for dusting

salt and freshly ground black pepper

2 tbsp sunflower oil

1 onion, finely chopped

1 courgette (zucchini), finely diced

75 g / 3 oz / 1 cup button mushrooms, cleaned

150 g / 5 oz / 1 ½ cups peas

500 ml / 18 fl. oz / 2 cups beef stock

150 g / 5 oz prepared shortcrust pastry

1 small egg white, beaten briefly

METHOD

1. Dust the beef with the flour and season with salt and pepper. Heat the oil in a large casserole dish set over a moderate heat until hot.

2. Seal the beef, in batches, until golden brown, then remove from the dish. Reduce the heat under the dish and add the onion and courgette, sweating them for 4–5 minutes.

3. Add the mushrooms and peas and continue to cook for 2 minutes before adding the beef again.

4. Cover with the stock, stir well and bring to a simmer. Cook gently for 50–55 minutes until the beef is tender.

5. Season to taste, then spoon into a round baking dish. Preheat the oven to 180°C (160°C fan) / 350F / gas 4.

6. Roll out the pastry on a lightly floured surface to ½ cm (¼ in) thickness; drape over the dish and seal against the rim, then cut away any excess.

7. Cut a small hole in the middle of the pastry. Brush the top with beaten egg white and bake for 25–30 minutes until golden.

8. Remove from the oven and leave to stand briefly before serving.

MEAT PIES

Beef and Ale Pie

SERVES 6

PREPARATION TIME **10–15 MINUTES**

COOKING TIME **1 HOUR 35–45 MINUTES**

INGREDIENTS

3 tbsp sunflower oil
salt and freshly ground black pepper
750 g / 1 lb 10 oz / 5 cups chuck steak,
    trimmed and cubed
1 onion, finely chopped
500 ml / 18 fl. oz / 2 cups good-quality ale
    or bitter
500 ml / 18 fl. oz / 2 cups beef stock
350 g / 12 oz ready-made shortcrust pastry
a large handful of frozen peas
a little plain (all-purpose) flour, for dusting
1 large egg, beaten

METHOD

1. Preheat the oven to 180°C (160°C fan) / 35(/ gas 4.

2. Heat the oil in a large casserole dish set over a moderate heat until hot. Season the beef steak and seal, in batches, until golde brown all over.

3. Remove the beef from the dish and reduce the heat, then pour off all the fat except for 1 tbsp worth. Add the onion and sauté for 3–4 minutes, then return the beef to the dish.

4. Add the ale and let it bubble up, then add the stock. Bring to a simmer and for 40–45 minutes until the beef is tender.

5. Roll out the pastry on a lightly floured surface to 1 cm (½ in) thickness. Use it to cover the base and sides of a 20 cm (8 in) p dish, letting the excess overhang the sides by 5–6 cm (3 in).

6. Prick the base with a fork, then use a slotte spoon to fill with the beef and ale filling. Sprinkle over the peas.

7. Fold the overhanging pastry back over the rim, folding and pleating around the edge c the dish.

8. Brush the top of the pastry with beaten egg then bake for 40–45 minutes until golden and cooked.

Beef and Onion Pie

SERVES 4

PREPARATION TIME 15 MINUTES

COOKING TIME 1 HOUR 40–50 MINUTES

INGREDIENTS

1 tbsp sunflower oil
salt and freshly ground black pepper
600 g / 1 lb 5 oz / 4 cups braising steak, diced
2 onions, roughly chopped
125 ml / 4 ½ fl. oz / ½ cup red wine
500 ml / 18 fl. oz / 2 cups beef stock
1 small bunch of flat-leaf parsley, chopped
150 g / 5 oz prepared hot water pastry
a little plain (all-purpose) flour, for dusting
1 small egg, beaten

METHOD

1. Heat the oil in a ovenproof saucepan set over a moderate heat until hot. Season the steak and seal in the pan until golden brown all over.

2. Remove from the pan and reduce the heat a little. Add the onion and sauté for 4–5 minutes, then deglaze the pan with the red wine.

3. Return the steak to the pan and cover with the stock. Bring to a simmer and cook for 40–45 minutes until tender, then stir in the parsley.

4. Preheat the oven to 180°C (160°C fan) / 350F / gas 4. Roll out the pastry on a lightly floured surface to 1 cm (½ in) thickness and drape over the top of the pan, cutting away some of the excess.

5. Reroll the excess pastry and cut into thin strips. Lay over top of the pastry, covering the middle in an interwoven, crosshatch pattern.

6. Brush with beaten egg, then place in the oven and bake for 30–35 minutes.

7. Remove from the oven and leave to stand for 5 minutes before serving.

TOP TIP

Scrape the base of the pan well after adding the wine to help dislodge any residue.

Beef Wellington

SERVES 4

PREPARATION TIME 20 MINUTES

COOKING TIME 45–50 MINUTES

INGREDIENTS

2 tbsp sunflower oil

650 g / 1 lb 7 oz piece of beef fillet, trimmed

salt and freshly ground black pepper

2 tbsp olive oil

1 clove of garlic, minced

1 shallot, finely chopped

150 g / 5 oz / 2 cups chestnut mushrooms,
    finely chopped

½ lemon, juiced

a small bunch of flat-leaf parsley, finely chopped

300 g / 10 ½ oz prepared shortcrust pastry

a little plain (all-purpose) flour, for dusting

1 large egg, beaten

METHOD

1. Preheat the oven to 180°C (160°C fan) / 350°F
   / gas 4.

2. Heat the sunflower oil in a large frying pan
   set over a moderate heat until hot. Season
   the beef and seal until golden all over, then
   remove from the pan.

3. Heat the olive oil in a large frying pan
   over a medium heat until hot. Sweat the
   garlic and shallot for 3–4 minutes until
   softened, then add the mushrooms.

4. Continue to cook, stirring occasionally, for
   5 minutes, then season to taste with lemon
   juice, add the parsley and season again.

5. Roll out the pastry on a lightly floured
   surface into a rectangle approximately
   25 cm x 15 cm (10 in x 7 in) and 1 cm (½ in)
   thick. Spread half of the mushrooms over
   the base and sit the beef fillet on top.

6. Spoon the rest of the mushrooms over the
   beef fillet, then bring the pastry over and
   around the beef to seal. Decorate the top of
   the pastry with any leftover pastry strips.

7. Transfer to a baking tray and brush with the
   beaten egg. Bake for 18–22 minutes for
   medium-rare and another 5–7 minutes
   for medium.

8. Remove from the oven and leave to rest for
   at least 5 minutes before slicing and serving.

ourgette and eef Cottage ie

RVES 4–6

EPARATION TIME **15 MINUTES**

OKING TIME **1 HOUR 20–30 MINUTES**

GREDIENTS

sp olive oil

ion, finely chopped

ick of celery, finely chopped

0 g / 1 lb 5 oz / 4 cups beef mince

sp Worcestershire sauce

ml / 13 fl. oz / 1 ½ cups beef stock

g / 2 lb 4 oz / 6 ⅔ cups floury potatoes, peeled and diced evenly

g / 3 oz / ⅓ cup unsalted butter, softened

t and freshly ground black pepper

g / 3 oz / ¾ cup Parmesan, grated

METHOD

1. Heat the olive oil in a large casserole dish set over a medium heat until hot. Sweat the onion and celery for 4–5 minutes, stirring occasionally, until softened.

2. Add the sliced courgettes and continue to cook for 3–4 minutes.

3. Add the beef mince and brown all over, then add the Worcestershire sauce and beef stock. Bring to a simmer, then cook over a reduced heat for 15–20 minutes.

4. Meanwhile, cook the potatoes in a large saucepan of boiling, salted water for 15–20 minutes until tender to the point of a knife.

5. Drain and leave to steam dry for a few minutes, then mash with the butter until smooth and season to taste.

6. Preheat the oven to 180°C (160°C fan) / 350F / gas 4 and spoon the beef and courgette mixture into the base of a baking dish.

7. Spread the mashed potato on top and sprinkle over the Parmesan, then bake for 40–45 minutes until golden on top.

8. Remove from the oven and leave to stand for a few minutes before serving.

Steak and Mushroom Pie

SERVES 6

PREPARATION TIME 15 MINUTES

COOKING TIME 1 HOUR 15–20 MINUTES

INGREDIENTS

55 ml / 2 fl. oz / ¼ cup sunflower oil

salt and freshly ground black pepper

1 kg / 2 lb 4 oz / 6 ⅔ cups stewing steak, trimmed and diced

1 tbsp plain (all-purpose) flour, plus extra for dusting

1 onion, finely chopped

150 g / 5 oz / 2 cups closed cap mushrooms, sliced

175 ml / 6 fl. oz / ¾ cup beer

750 ml / 1 pint 6 fl. oz / 3 cups beef stock

a small bunch of flat-leaf parsley, roughly chopped

250 g / 9 oz prepared puff pastry

1 large egg, beaten

METHOD

1. Heat the oil in a large casserole dish set over a moderate heat until hot. Season th steak and seal, in batches, until golden brown all over.

2. Remove the steak from the dish and pour any excess oil so that you have 2 tbsp left; sprinkle the flour over the sealed steak.

3. Add the onions and mushrooms. Sauté for 3–4 minutes, stirring occasionally, then deglaze with the beer and return the stea to the dish.

4. Cover with the stock and bring to a simme Cook at a steady simmer for 45–50 minute until tender, then stir through the parsley and season to taste.

5. Preheat the oven to 190°C (170°C fan) / 37 / gas 5 and spoon the beef and mushroom into a rectangular baking dish.

6. Roll out the pastry on a lightly floured surface into a rectangle slightly larger tha the baking dish; drape over the top of the beef filling and seal against the rim.

7. Score a light pattern on the top of the past using a knife. Brush with beaten egg and bake for 20–25 minutes until golden on top

8. Remove from the oven and leave to stand f 5 minutes before serving.

Steak and Kidney Pie

SERVES 6

PREPARATION TIME 15–20 MINUTES

COOKING TIME 2 HOURS 15 MINUTES

INGREDIENTS

tbsp sunflower oil

750 g / 1 lb 10 oz / 5 cups stewing steak, trimmed and evenly diced

onion, chopped

250 g / 9 oz / 1 ⅔ cups lamb's kidneys, cored and diced

tbsp plain (all-purpose) flour, plus extra for dusting

600 ml / 1 pint 10 fl. oz / 3 ½ cups beef stock

dash of Worcestershire sauce

salt and freshly ground black pepper

small bunch of flat-leaf parsley, finely chopped

200 g / 7 oz prepared flaky pastry

small egg, beaten

METHOD

1. Heat the oil in a large casserole dish set over a moderate heat until hot.

2. Season the steak and seal in batches, until golden all over, then remove from the dish and drain on kitchen paper.

3. Reduce the heat under the dish and sauté the onion in the accumulated oil for 3–4 minutes until golden.

4. Return the steak to the dish along with the kidneys and flour. Stir well and cook for 1 minute, then cover with the stock and Worcestershire sauce.

5. Bring to a simmer and cook steadily for 1 ¼–½ hours, uncovered, until the steak is tender.

6. Adjust the seasoning to taste and stir through the parsley, then spoon into a square baking dish. Preheat the oven to 220°C (200°C fan) / 425F / gas 7.

7. Roll out the pastry on a lightly floured surface into a rectangle slightly larger than the dish, then drape over the beef filling. Seal against the edges and cut away any excess.

8. Brush the top with the beaten egg and bore a small hole in the centre. Bake for 25–30 minutes until golden and risen.

Pork and Cider Pie

SERVES 4

PREPARATION TIME **15–20 MINUTES**

COOKING TIME **1 HOUR 45–50 MINUTES**

INGREDIENTS

3 tbsp sunflower oil

salt and freshly ground black pepper

650 g / 1 lb 7 oz / 4 ⅓ cups pork shoulder,
    trimmed and diced

2 large onions, finely sliced

2 large Bramley apples, cored, peeled and sliced

250 ml / 9 fl. oz / 1 cup cider

550 ml / 1 pint / 2 ¼ cups ham stock

200 g / 7 oz prepared hot water pastry

a little plain (all-purpose) flour, for dusting

1 small egg, beaten

METHOD

1. Preheat the oven to 180°C (160°C fan) / 3?
   / gas 4.

2. Heat the oil in a large saucepan set over a
   moderate heat until hot. Season the pork
   then seal in batches until golden brown.

3. Remove from the saucepan and reduce th?
   heat a little, then add the onion and apple?
   Sweat for 5 minutes, then deglaze with
   the cider.

4. Add the pork back to the saucepan and co?
   with the stock. Bring to a simmer and bra?
   gently for 40–45 minutes until tender, the?
   season and strain into a large, round
   baking dish.

5. Roll out the pastry on a lightly floured
   surface to 1 cm (½ in) thickness; cut it to
   shape and lay over the pork filling, then
   brush the top with beaten egg.

6. Bake for 35–45 minutes until golden and
   cooked through, then remove from the
   oven and leave to stand for 5 minutes
   before serving.

TOP TIP

Strain the pork filling well
before spooning into the
dish to prevent a soggy
pastry crust.

Pork Pie

SERVES 8

PREPARATION TIME 10 MINUTES

COOKING TIME 2 HOURS 0–15 MINUTES

INGREDIENTS

500 g / 1 lb / 3 cups diced pork shoulder
500 g / 1 lb 5 oz / 4 cups pork mince
2 tsp Worcestershire sauce
2 tsp ground allspice
1 tsp dried sage
Salt and freshly ground black pepper
500 g / 1 lb prepared hot water pastry
A little plain (all-purpose) flour, for dusting
1 egg, lightly beaten

METHOD

1. Heat the oil in a large casserole dish set over a moderate heat until hot.

2. Season the steak and seal in batches until golden all over, then remove from the dish and drain on kitchen paper.

3. Reduce the heat under the dish and sauté the onion in the accumulated oil for 3–4 minutes until golden.

4. Return the steak to the dish along with the kidneys and flour. Stir well and cook for 1 minute, then cover with the stock and Worcestershire sauce.

5. Bring to a simmer and cook steadily for 1 ¼–½ hours, uncovered, until the steak is tender.

6. Adjust the seasoning to taste and stir through the parsley, then spoon into a square baking dish. Preheat the oven to 220°C (200°C fan) / 425F / gas 7.

7. Roll out the pastry on a lightly floured surface into a rectangle slightly larger than the dish, then drape over the beef filling. Seal against the edges and cut away any excess.

8. Brush the top with the beaten egg and bore a small hole in the centre. Bake for 25–30 minutes until golden and risen.

Lamb and Onion Pie

SERVES 6

PREPARATION TIME 15 MINUTES

COOKING TIME 3 HOURS 15 MINUTES

INGREDIENTS

300 ml / 10 ½ fl. oz / 1 ¼ cups lamb stock
600 g/ 1 lb 5 oz lamb shoulder, in large chunks
3 onions, sliced

For the topping:
450 g / 1 lb / 4 cups floury potatoes,
    peeled and cubed
100 ml / 3 ½ fl. oz / ½ cup milk
50 g / 1 ¾ oz / ¼ cup butter
3 tbsp flat leaf parsley, leaves only
25 g / 1 oz / ⅓ cup breadcrumbs

METHOD

1. Preheat the oven to 150°C (130° fan) / 300F
   gas 2 and bring the stock to the boil.

2. Mix the lamb and onions together in a cast
   iron casserole dish and season well with
   salt and pepper. Pour over the hot stock,
   then cover the dish and transfer to the ove
   for 3 hours.

3. Thirty minutes before the end of the cookin
   time, remove the lid so that the onions take
   on some colour.

4. Boil the potatoes in salted water for
   12 minutes, or until they are tender, then
   drain well. Return the potatoes to the
   saucepan and add the milk, butter and
   parsley, then mash until smooth.

5. Remove the lamb from the oven and
   increase the temperature to 200°C
   (180°C fan) / 400F / gas 6.

6. Shred the lamb into smaller chunks with
   2 forks and stir it back into the onions.

7. Top the lamb with the mashed potato and
   sprinkle with breadcrumbs, then bake in
   the oven for 15 minutes or until the top is
   golden brown.

TOP TIP
Replace the potatoes with sweet potatoes for a sweeter topping.

Tagine Pot Pie

SERVES 4

PREPARATION TIME **15 MINUTES**

COOKING TIME **1 HOUR 40-50 MINUTES**

INGREDIENTS

tbsp olive oil

salt and freshly ground black pepper

0 g / 1 lb 10 oz / 5 cups lamb shoulder, diced

onion, finely chopped

carrots, peeled and diced

bsp harissa paste

0 ml / 18 fl. oz / 2 cups lamb stock

bsp white sesame seeds

0 g / 7 oz prepared shortcrust pastry

ttle plain (all-purpose) flour, for dusting

arge egg yolk

mall handful of mint leaves, to garnish

METHOD

1. Heat the olive oil in a large casserole dish set over a medium heat until hot. Season the lamb and seal in batches until golden brown, then remove from the dish.

2. Reduce the heat slightly, then add the onion, carrot and a little salt. Sweat for 5-6 minutes until softened.

3. Stir through the harissa and return the lamb to the dish. Cover with the stock and bring to a simmer.

4. Cook gently for 50-60 minutes until the lamb is tender. Season to taste, then spoon into a round baking dish and top with half the sesame seeds.

5. Preheat the oven to 180°C (160°C fan) / 350F / gas 4. Roll out the pastry on a lightly floured surface to 1 cm (½ in) thickness, then drape over the baking dish.

6. Seal well against the rim, cutting away any excess.

7. Beat the egg yolk with 1 tbsp of water and brush over the pastry and rim. Make a few incisions in the pastry with a sharp knife and top with the remaining sesame seeds.

8. Bake for 25-30 minutes until the pastry is golden and cooked; garnish with mint leaves before serving.

Bacon and Egg Pie

SERVES 4

PREPARATION TIME 25 MINUTES

COOKING TIME 40 MINUTES

INGREDIENTS

450 g / 1 lb / 3 cups floury potatoes,
    peeled and sliced
2 large eggs
4 rashers of back bacon, chopped
150 ml / 5 fl. oz / ⅔ cup double (heavy) cream
salt and freshly ground black pepper
200 g / 7 oz prepared shortcrust pastry
a little plain (all-purpose) flour, for dusting

METHOD

1. Cook the potato slices in a large saucepan
   salted, boiling water for 12–15 minutes un
   tender to the point of a knife.

2. Meanwhile, cook the eggs in a separate
   saucepan of boiling water for 12 minutes,
   then drain and refresh in iced water.

3. Drain the potato when ready and leave to
   steam dry for a few minutes. Peel and cho
   the eggs and combine with the potato
   slices, bacon, cream and seasoning in a
   mixing bowl.

4. Divide the mixture between 4 individual
   ramekins and arrange on a baking tray.

5. Preheat the oven to 160°C (140°C fan) / 32⁵
   / gas 3.

6. Roll out the pastry on a lightly floured
   surface to 1 cm (½ in) thickness. Cut out
   4 rounds and drape over the filling in
   the ramekins.

7. Seal the pastry against the ramekins by
   pushing against the edges with your thumb
   Bore a small hole in the centres.

8. Bake for 20–25 minutes until the pastry is
   golden and cooked through. Remove to a
   wire rack to cool before serving.

Shepherd's Pie

SERVES 6

PREPARATION TIME 25 MINUTES

COOKING TIME 50–60 MINUTES

INGREDIENTS

tbsp sunflower oil

large green pepper, deseeded and finely diced

onion, finely chopped

g / 1 lb 2 oz / 3 ⅓ cups lamb mince

g / 3 oz / 1 ½ cups baby spinach, washed

tsp Worcestershire sauce

ml / 9 fl. oz / 1 cup lamb stock

kg / 2 lb 4 oz / 6 ⅔ cups floury potatoes, peeled and cut into chunks

ourgettes (zucchinis), cut into large chunks

t and freshly ground black pepper

g / 3 ½ oz / 1 cup Cheddar, grated

ew sprigs of thyme, to garnish

METHOD

1. Heat the oil in a large casserole dish set over a medium heat, then add the pepper and onion and sweat for 6–8 minutes.

2. Increase the heat and add the lamb mince. Leave to brown for 2–3 minutes, then stir well.

3. Add the spinach and Worcestershire sauce. Stir well and cover with the stock, then cook at a simmer for 15 minutes.

4. Meanwhile, cook the potatoes in a large saucepan of salted, boiling water for 15–20 minutes until tender. Add the courgette chunks to the water 5 minutes before the potato is ready.

5. Drain well and mash with seasoning until smooth. Preheat the oven to 190°C (170°C fan) / 375F / gas 5 and spoon the lamb into an oval baking dish.

6. Top with the mashed potato and courgette, then smooth the top and sprinkle over the cheese.

7. Bake for 25–30 minutes until golden on top. Remove from the oven and leave to stand for 5 minutes, then garnish with thyme and serve.

Lamb and Mint Pie

SERVES 4

PREPARATION TIME **15 MINUTES**

COOKING TIME **50–60 MINUTES**

INGREDIENTS

3 tbsp sunflower oil
salt and freshly ground black pepper
600 g / 1 lb 5 oz / 4 cups lamb neck fillet,
    trimmed and diced
1 large carrot, peeled and sliced
1 onion, chopped
1 fennel bulb, trimmed and sliced
1 red pepper, deseeded and diced
2 tsp dried mint
250 ml / 9 fl. oz / 1 cup lamb stock
150 g / 5 oz prepared shortcrust pastry
a little plain (all-purpose) flour, for dusting

METHOD

1. Preheat the oven to 190°C (170°C fan) / 37
   / gas 5. Heat the oil in a casserole dish set
   over a moderate heat until hot.

2. Season the lamb and seal in batches until
   golden brown, then remove from the dish
   and reduce the heat a little.

3. Add the carrot, onion and fennel and swea
   for 4–5 minutes, stirring occasionally.

4. Add the pepper and 1 tsp of dried mint,
   stirring well, then return the lamb and cov
   with the stock.

5. Bring to a simmer and cook gently for
   15 minutes, then season and spoon into a
   20 cm (8 in) round baking dish.

6. Roll out the pastry on a lightly floured
   surface into a 22 cm (9 in) round,
   approximately ½ cm (¼ in) thick. Drape ove
   the baking dish and seal against the rim,
   cutting away any excess.

7. Make incisions across the pastry before
   baking for 20–25 minutes until golden.
   Remove to a wire rack to cool before
   garnishing with the rest of the dried mint.

Lamb, Pea and Potato Pie

RVES 6

EPARATION TIME 20 MINUTES

OKING TIME 1 HOUR 5–10 MINUTES

GREDIENTS

bsp sunflower oil

nion, finely chopped

loves of garlic, minced

lt and freshly ground black pepper

0 g / 1 lb 5 oz / 4 cups lamb mince

5 ml / 4 ½ fl. oz / ½ cup red wine

0 ml / 18 fl. oz / 2 cups lamb stock

0 g / 1 lb / 3 cups new potatoes, sliced

0 g / 5 oz / 1 ½ cups frozen peas

5 g / 8 oz prepared puff pastry

ittle plain (all-purpose) flour, for dusting

arge egg, beaten

METHOD

1. Heat the oil in a large casserole dish set over a medium heat until hot. Add the onion, garlic and a little salt, sweating for 5–6 minutes until softened.

2. Increase the heat a little and add the lamb mince. Brown well, breaking it up with a wooden spoon.

3. Once browned, deglaze with the red wine and cover with the stock, then bring to a simmer.

4. Stir in the potatoes and cook steadily for 20–25 minutes, then add the peas and season to taste.

5. Spoon into a large, rectangular baking dish and preheat the oven to 190°C (170°C fan) / 375F / gas 5.

6. Roll out the pastry on a lightly floured surface to ½ cm (¼ in) thickness. Drape over the baking dish and seal against the edges.

7. Trim any excess pastry and brush the top with the beaten egg, then score a light pattern in the pastry using a sharp knife.

8. Bake for 25–30 minutes until golden and puffed before serving.

TOP TIP

When deglazing the dish, scrape the base well to dislodge as any residue.

Lamb and Apricot Pie

SERVES 6

PREPARATION TIME 25 MINUTES

COOKING TIME 2 HOURS 5–10 MINUTES

INGREDIENTS

400 g / 14 oz prepared shortcrust pastry
a little plain (all-purpose) flour, for dusting
3 tbsp sunflower oil
750 g / 1 lb 10 oz / 5 cups lamb neck fillet,
    trimmed and cubed
1 onion, finely chopped
salt and freshly ground black pepper
2 tsp ras el hanout
1 tsp paprika
225 g / 8 oz / 1 ½ cups dried apricots, chopped
500 ml / 18 fl. oz / 2 cups lamb stock
1 small egg, beaten

METHOD

1. Roll out two-thirds of the pastry on a light
   floured surface to 1 cm (½ in) thickness ar
   use to line the base and sides of a 20 cm
   (8 in) springform cake tin.

2. Trim any excess pastry and prick the base
   with a fork, then chill.

3. Heat the oil in a large casserole dish set
   over a moderate heat until hot. Season the
   lamb and seal in batches until golden
   all over.

4. Remove the lamb from the dish and reduce
   the heat slightly, then add the onion and a
   little salt and sweat for 4–5 minutes.

5. Stir in the spices and apricots, then return
   the lamb to the dish. Cover with the stock
   and bring to a simmer.

6. Cook gently for 1 hour 5–10 minutes until t
   lamb is very tender. Use a couple of forks
   shred the lamb and season to taste.

7. Strain the liquid from the lamb and apricot
   then spoon the filling into the chilled pastr
   Preheat the oven to 180°C (160°C fan) / 350
   / gas 4.

8. Roll out the remaining pastry to 1 cm (½ in
   thickness. Drape over the cake tin and sea
   against the side of the lined pastry.

9. Brush the top with beaten egg, then bake f
   40–45 minutes until golden and cooked
   before serving.

Game Pie

GREDIENTS

sp sunflower oil

: and freshly ground black pepper

g / 1 lb / 3 cups venison loin,
trimmed and diced

g / 12 oz / 2 ⅓ cups skinless pigeon or grouse
breast, trimmed and diced

sp Cognac or brandy

mall bunch of flat-leaf parsley, chopped

g / 12 oz prepared flaky pastry, divided in two

rge egg, beaten

METHOD

1. Preheat the oven to 180°C (160°C fan) / 350F / gas 4. Heat the oil in a large casserole dish set over a moderate heat until hot.

2. Season the meats and seal in batches until golden brown, then remove from the dish. Deglaze the dish with the Cognac, then tip the liquid and meat into a food processor.

3. Add the parsley and seasoning and pulse until the mixture comes together.

4. Roll out a piece of the pastry on a lightly floured surface into a 30 cm (12 in) round approximately ½ cm (¼ in) thick.

5. Lift onto a baking tray and top with the game mixture, leaving a 2 cm (1 in) border all the way around.

6. Roll out the other piece of pastry to the same dimensions as the first piece. Brush the border of the pastry base with beaten egg, then drape the other round of pastry over the filling.

7. Seal the edges and brush the top with the rest of the beaten egg, then bake for 40–45 minutes until golden brown.

8. Remove from the oven and leave to cool before serving.

Pheasant Pie

SERVES **4**

PREPARATION TIME **20 MINUTES**

COOKING TIME **45–50 MINUTES**

INGREDIENTS

2 tbsp unsalted butter

2 tbsp plain (all-purpose) flour,
plus extra for dusting

600 ml / 1 pint 2 fl. oz / 2 ½ cups whole
(full-fat) milk

1 bay leaf

450 g / 1 lb / 3 cups skinless pheasant breast, diced

150 g / 5 oz / 2 cups morel mushrooms, cleaned

225 g / 8 oz prepared puff pastry

a little plain (all-purpose) flour, for dusting

1 large egg, beaten

salt and freshly ground black pepper

METHOD

1. Melt the butter in a large saucepan set ov
   a medium heat until hot. Whisk in the flou
   and cook until you have a golden roux.

2. Add the milk in a slow, steady stream,
   whisking constantly, until you have a smo
   sauce, then add the bay leaf and pheasan

3. Simmer for 10 minutes, stirring
   occasionally, then add the morels and
   season to taste. Spoon into 4 individual
   ramekins and arrange on a baking tray.

4. Preheat the oven to 190°C (170°C fan) / 37
   / gas 5.

5. Roll out the pastry on a lightly floured
   surface to ½ cm (¼ in) thickness and cut c
   4 rounds that will fit as lids on top of the
   ramekins.

6. Drape the rounds over the filling and seal
   against the rims, using a little beaten egg
   the rim to help seal them.

7. Brush the tops of the pastry with more
   beaten egg and bake for 20–25 minutes u
   golden and puffed.

8. Remove from the oven and leave to stand
   5 minutes before serving.

Rabbit Pie

SERVES 6–8

PREPARATION TIME **25 MINUTES**

COOKING TIME **2 HOURS 20–30 MINUTES**

INGREDIENTS

tbsp sunflower oil

Salt and freshly ground black pepper

750 g / 1 lb 10 oz / 5 cups rabbit loin, diced

cloves of garlic, minced

tbsp Cognac or brandy

Dash of Worcestershire sauce

500 g / 9 oz / 1 ²⁄₃ cup foie gras, de-veined and cut into chunks

tbsp green peppercorns in brine, drained

large egg yolks, beaten

METHOD

1. Heat the oil in a large casserole dish set over a moderate heat until hot. Season the rabbit and seal in batches until golden all over, then transfer to a food processor.

2. Add the garlic, Cognac and Worcestershire sauce and blitz until combined.

3. Take two-thirds of the pastry and roll out on a lightly floured surface into a 30 cm (12 in) round, approximately 1 cm (½ in) thick.

4. Use it to line a rimmed 20 cm (8 in) pie dish. Spoon half of the rabbit mixture into the base, then top with the foie gras and peppercorns.

5. Pack the rest of the rabbit mixture on top and smooth with the back of a tablespoon. Roll out the remaining pastry into a 22 cm (9 in) round, approximately 1 cm (½ in) thick.

6. Drape over the filling and crimp against the other piece of pastry using a little water to help. Preheat the oven to 160°C (140°C fan) / 325F / gas 3.

7. Bake the pie for 1 ½ hours, then remove from the oven and carefully loosen the pie from the dish and invert onto a baking tray.

8. Score a pattern on the pastry, then brush with the remaining egg yolk and return to the oven for 30 minutes to brown.

9. Leave to cool for 5 minutes before serving.

Poultry Pies

Chicken and Mushroom Pie

SERVES 4

PREPARATION TIME **15 MINUTES**

COOKING TIME **40–50 MINUTES**

INGREDIENTS

2 tbsp sunflower oil
1 large leek, sliced
salt and freshly ground black pepper
2 large skinless chicken breasts, diced
250 g / 9 oz / 3 cups closed cup mushrooms,
    roughly chopped
500 ml / 18 fl. oz / 2 cups chicken stock
110 g / 4 oz / 1 cup frozen peas
2 sheets of filo pastry
2 tbsp unsalted butter, melted

METHOD

1. Preheat the oven to 190°C (170°C fan) / 375°F
   / gas 5 and heat the oil in a saucepan set
   over a medium heat.

2. Add the leek and some seasoning and sweat
   for 4–5 minutes, stirring occasionally.

3. Add the chicken and mushrooms and cook
   for a further 4–5 minutes, then cover with
   the stock.

4. Bring to a simmer and cook steadily for
   8–10 minutes, then stir through the peas
   and season to taste.

5. Spoon into individual ramekins. Use a sharp
   knife to cut out rounds of filo pastry.

6. Wet the rims of the ramekins with melted
   butter and top with the rounds of pastry,
   then brush the tops with more melted butter.

7. Bake for 15–20 minutes until the pastry is
   golden and cooked, then remove from the
   oven and leave to stand briefly before serving.

TOP TIP

Keep the filo pastry under a damp tea towel to prevent it from drying out.

Curried Chicken Pie

SERVES 4

PREPARATION TIME 20 MINUTES

COOKING TIME 40–45 MINUTES

INGREDIENTS

- tbsp unsalted butter
- large leek, sliced
- cloves of garlic, minced
- salt and freshly ground black pepper
- tbsp Madras curry powder
- small skinless chicken breasts, diced
- 375 ml / 13 fl. oz / 1 ½ cups chicken stock
- 375 ml / 13 fl. oz / 1 ½ cups double (heavy) cream
- small handful of flat-leaf parsley, finely chopped
- 250 g / 9 oz prepared puff pastry
- little plain (all-purpose) flour, for dusting
- small egg, beaten

METHOD

1. Preheat the oven to 180°C (160°C fan) / 350F / gas 4. Melt the butter in a large saucepan set over a medium heat.

2. Add the leek, garlic and a little salt and sweat for 6–7 minutes, stirring occasionally, until softened.

3. Add the curry powder. Stir well, and cook for 1 minute, then add the chicken.

4. Cover with the stock and bring to a simmer. Cook for 5 minutes, then stir through the cream, parsley and some seasoning.

5. Spoon into a large cast-iron pan or baking dish. Roll out the pastry on a lightly floured surface into a round approximately 1 cm (½ in) thick.

6. Drape over the filling and seal against the inside edge of the pan or dish. Cut away any excess and bore a small hole in the middle.

7. Brush with beaten egg and bake for 20–25 minutes until puffed and golden, then serve.

TOP TIP

Boring a hole will help steam to escape from the pastry and aid in rising.

Chicken and Lemon Pie

SERVES 4

PREPARATION TIME 25 MINUTES

COOKING TIME 1 HOUR 20–25 MINUTES

INGREDIENTS

350 g / 12 oz prepared shortcrust pastry
a little plain (all-purpose) flour, for dusting
3 tbsp olive oil
1 onion, finely chopped
2 cloves of garlic, minced
salt and freshly ground black pepper
4 large skinless chicken breasts, diced
150 g / 5 oz / 1 cup pitted green olives
150 g / 5 oz / 3 cups chopped kale
1 preserved lemon, drained and chopped
a few sprigs of rosemary, finely chopped

METHOD

1. Preheat the oven to 160°C (140°C fan) / 32 / gas 3. Roll out two-thirds of the pastry o a lightly floured surface to ½ cm (¼ in) thickness.

2. Use the pastry to line a 20 cm (8 in) pie dis cutting away the excess and pressing well into the base and sides.

3. Prick the base with a fork, then chill until ready to fill.

4. Heat the oil in a large casserole dish set over a medium heat until hot. Add the onion, garlic and a little salt, sweating for 5–6 minutes until softened.

5. Add the chicken, olives, kale and preserve lemon and continue to cook for a further 7–8 minutes, stirring occasionally, then season.

6. Stir through most of the rosemary, then spoon the filling into the lined pastry with slotted spoon. Roll out the remaining past to the same thickness as before.

7. Drape over the filling and crimp against the inside of the lined pastry. Cut away the excess and cut out a small hole in the middle.

8. Bake for 55–60 minutes until the pastry is golden and cooked. Garnish with the remaining rosemary sprinkled on top, then serve.

Chicken, Ham and Leek Pie

SERVES 4

PREPARATION TIME **15 MINUTES**

COOKING TIME **40–45 MINUTES**

INGREDIENTS

- tbsp unsalted butter
- small carrots, peeled and diced
- large skinless chicken breasts, diced
- g / 5 oz / 1 cup cooked gammon steak, cubed
- ml / 13 fl. oz / 1 ½ cups ham stock
- ml / 9 fl. oz / 1 cup double (heavy) cream
- g / 5 oz / 1 ½ cups frozen peas
- g / 5 oz prepared puff pastry
- little plain (all-purpose) flour, for dusting
- large egg, beaten

METHOD

1. Melt the butter in a large saucepan set over a medium heat until hot. Add the carrot and sweat for 3–4 minutes.

2. Add the chicken and gammon steak, then cook for a further 4–5 minutes, stirring occasionally, before covering with the stock.

3. Bring to a simmer and cook for another 5 minutes, then stir in the cream and peas. Simmer for 2 minutes, then pour into a round pie dish.

4. Preheat the oven to 180°C (160°C fan) / 350F / gas 4.

5. Roll out the pastry on a lightly floured surface into a 1 cm (½ in) thick round. Drape over the filling in the dish and seal against the inside rim, cutting away any excess pastry.

6. Brush the top with beaten egg and score a crosshatch pattern using a sharp knife. Bake for 20–25 minutes until golden and risen, then serve.

TOP TIP

Adjust the amount of cream as necessary to get the right consistency.

Duck and Sweet Potato Pie

SERVES 4–6

PREPARATION TIME **15 MINUTES**

COOKING TIME **2 HOURS 5–10 MINUTES**

INGREDIENTS

4 duck legs on the bone
salt and freshly ground black pepper
2 tbsp sunflower oil
750 g / 1 lb 10 oz / 5 cups sweet potatoes,
    peeled and cut into chunks
110 g / 4 oz / ½ cup unsalted butter, cubed
75 g / 3 oz / 1 cup Parmesan, grated
75 g / 3 oz / 1 cup fresh breadcrumbs

METHOD

1. Preheat the oven to 190°C (170°C fan) / 3?° / gas 5. Place the duck legs on a baking tr and prick the skin with a wooden skewer.

2. Season with salt and pepper, then drizzle with sunflower oil. Roast for 1 hour 20–30 minutes until the skin is golden and crisp.

3. Remove from the oven and leave to rest, covered loosely with aluminium foil, for 15 minutes.

4. Meanwhile, cook the sweet potatoes in a large saucepan of salted, boiling water fo 15–20 minutes until tender to the point of a knife.

5. Drain well and leave to cool slightly, then mash with the butter and seasoning until smooth.

6. Shred the duck meat from the legs, discarding the skin and bones, and arran in the base of an oval baking dish.

7. Top with the sweet potato mash and sprin over the Parmesan and breadcrumbs.

8. Bake for 30–35 minutes until golden on to then serve immediately.

TOP TIP
The sweet potato chunks should be evenly cut into 5 cm (2 in) cubes.

uck Pie

KES 4

PARATION TIME 20 MINUTES

)KING TIME 1 HOUR 40–45 MINUTES

GREDIENTS

sp sunflower oil

rge onions, chopped

ove of garlic, finely chopped

ick of celery, finely chopped

edium carrots, peeled and chopped

rge duck legs

p Worcestershire sauce

ml / 1 pint 6 fl. oz / 3 cups chicken stock

g / 10 ½ oz prepared puff pastry

tle plain (all-purpose) flour, for dusting

rge egg, beaten

and freshly ground black pepper

METHOD

1. Heat the oil in a large casserole dish set over a medium heat until hot. Add the onion, garlic, celery, carrot and a little salt and sweat for 7–8 minutes until softened.

2. Add the duck legs and Worcestershire sauce and cook for 2 minutes, stirring occasionally, before covering with the stock.

3. Bring to a simmer and cook gently, covered, for 1 hour, then remove the duck legs and shred the meat back into the vegetables and gravy.

4. Preheat the oven to 190°C (170°C fan) / 375F / gas 5. Roll out half of the pastry on a lightly floured surface to 1 cm (½ in) thickness and use it to line the base and sides of a round baking dish.

5. Trim any excess overhanging pastry, then spoon the duck meat and vegetables into the pastry.

6. Roll out the remaining pastry and drape over the filing, sealing against the side of the lined pastry.

7. Brush with the beaten egg and bake for 25–30 minutes until golden and puffed, then serve.

TOP TIP

Use a slotted spoon to spoon the duck filling into the pastry.

Turkey Pie

MAKES 4

PREPARATION TIME 15–20 MINUTES

COOKING TIME 45–50 MINUTES

INGREDIENTS

1 kg / 2 lb 4 oz / 6 ⅔ cups floury potatoes,
    peeled and diced
4 medium Bramley apples, peeled,
    cored and diced
2 tbsp caster (superfine) sugar
75 g / 3 oz / ⅓ cup butter, softened
55 ml / 2 fl. oz / ¼ cup double (heavy) cream
salt and freshly ground black pepper
2 tbsp sunflower oil
4 large turkey breast escalopes
1 Braeburn apple, cored and finely diced

METHOD

1. Cook the potatoes in a large saucepan of
   salted, boiling water for 15–20 minutes u
   tender to the point of a knife.

2. Meanwhile, place the Bramley apples
   and sugar in a large saucepan with 2 tbsp
   of cold water.

3. Cover and cook over a medium heat until
   soft enough to break with a wooden spoo
   then remove from the heat and mash brie
   into a purée.

4. Drain the potatoes and leave to steam for
   few minutes, then mash with the butter,
   cream and seasoning.

5. Preheat the oven to 190°C (170°C fan) / 37
   / gas 5.

6. Heat the sunflower oil in a large frying pa
   set over a moderate heat until hot. Seaso
   the turkey escalopes and seal for 1 minut
   on both sides before removing from the p

7. Spoon the apple purée into the base of
   4 individual baking dishes. Top with the
   turkey and then a layer of mashed potato.

8. Sprinkle over the diced Braeburn apple
   and bake for 15 minutes before serving.

Turkey Leftover Pie

SERVES 8

PREPARATION TIME 20 MINUTES

COOKING TIME 1 HOUR 30–40 MINUTES

INGREDIENTS

400 g / 14 oz prepared hot water pastry
a little plain (all-purpose) flour, for dusting
450 g / 1 lb / 3 cups leftover turkey meat, sliced
225 g / 8 oz / 1 ½ cups leftover ham, sliced
225 g / 8 oz / 1 ½ cups leftover stuffing
110 g / 4 oz / ½ cup cranberry sauce
1 small egg, beaten
salt and freshly ground black pepper

METHOD

1. Preheat the oven to 160°C (140°C fan) / 325F / gas 3.

2. Roll out two-thirds of the pastry on a lightly floured surface to 1 cm (½ in) thickness and use it to line a 20 cm (8 in) springform cake tin.

3. Press well into the base and sides and trim the excess. Prick the base with a fork and fill with a combination of the leftover meats, stuffing and cranberry sauce.

4. Roll out the remaining pastry and drape over the filling. Seal against the side of the lined pastry, trimming away the excess.

5. Brush the top with beaten egg and bore a small hole in the middle, then bake for 1 hour 30–40 minutes until the pastry is golden and cooked.

6. Remove to a wire rack to cool before turning out and serving.

TOP TIP
Use a combination of turkey breast and leg meat for the best taste.

Fish and Seafood Pies

Smoked Salmon and Herb Pie

SERVES 6–8

PREPARATION TIME **25 MINUTES**

COOKING TIME **1 HOUR 15–20 MINUTES**

INGREDIENTS

750 g / 1 lb 10 oz / 5 cups smoked salmon fillet
225 ml / 8 fl. oz / 1 cup dry white wine
150 ml / 5 fl. oz / ⅔ cup water
1 bay leaf
6 small eggs
salt and freshly ground black pepper
350 g / 12 oz / 2 ⅓ cups cooked long-grain rice
a large bunch of chives
350 g / 12 oz prepared shortcrust pastry
a little plain (all-purpose) flour, for dusting

METHOD

1. Place the salmon fillet in a large saucepan and add the white wine, water and bay leaf. Bring to a simmer, cover and cook for 8–10 minutes until cooked through, then drain.

2. Preheat the oven to 180°C (160°C fan) / 350 / gas 4. Cook the eggs in a large saucepan boiling water for 10 minutes.

3. Drain the eggs and refresh in iced water. Flake the salmon into a large mixing bowl and season with salt and pepper.

4. Place the rice in a large mixing bowl. Finely chop half of the chives and stir into the rice with salt and pepper.

5. Roll out two-thirds of the pastry on a lightly floured surface into a large rectangle approximately 1 cm (½ in) thick and use it to line a 900 g / 2 lb rectangular loaf or baking tin.

6. Fill the base with half of the rice. Top with half of the salmon, then peel the eggs and lay down the middle of the salmon.

7. Top with more salmon and the remaining rice. Roll out the remaining pastry and drape over the filing, then crimp against the edge of the lined pastry.

8. Bake for 40–45 minutes until the pastry is golden and cooked through, then garnish with the remaining chives and serve.

almon and otato Pie

VES 6

EPARATION TIME **15–20 MINUTES**

)KING TIME **1 HOUR 5–15 MINUTES**

GREDIENTS

g / 14 oz / 2 ⅔ cups skinless salmon fillet,
diced

ml / 9 fl. oz / 1 cup fish stock

ay leaf

p dried dill

g / 1 lb 10 oz / 5 cups floury potatoes,
peeled and sliced

g / 12 oz prepared hot water pastry

ttle plain (all-purpose) flour, for dusting

rge egg, beaten

METHOD

1. Place the salmon fillet in a large saucepan
   and cover with the fish stock and 150 ml /
   5 fl. oz / ⅔ cup of water. Add the bay leaf
   and dill and bring to a simmer over a
   medium heat.

2. Cover and cook for 5–6 minutes until cooked
   through. Remove from the heat and strain
   the fish.

3. Preheat the oven to 180°C (160°C fan) / 350F
   / gas 4. Bring a large saucepan of salted
   water to the boil and cook the potato slices
   for 6–7 minutes until tender to the point of
   a knife.

4. Drain and leave to dry. Roll out two-thirds of
   the pastry on a lightly floured surface into a
   large round approximately 1 cm (½ in) thick.

5. Use the round of pastry to line the base and
   sides of a 20 cm (8 in) pie dish. Flake the
   cooked salmon and spoon onto the base,
   then top with the potato slices.

6. Roll out the remaining pastry to a round
   approximately 1 cm (½ in) thick. Drape over
   the filling and crimp against the edge of the
   pastry, then brush with the beaten egg.

7. Bake for 45–50 minutes until the pastry is
   golden and cooked, then serve.

Salmon and Prawn Pie

SERVES **4**

PREPARATION TIME **20 MINUTES**

COOKING TIME **35–40 MINUTES**

INGREDIENTS

2 tbsp olive oil

½ large leek, sliced

salt and freshly ground black pepper

450 g / 1 lb / 3 cups skinless salmon fillet, diced

300 g / 10 ½ oz / 2 cups whole prawns (shrimp),
    peeled and deveined

150 g / 5 oz / 1 cup mussels, cleaned with
    beards removed

a small bunch of thyme sprigs

125 ml / 4 ½ fl. oz / ½ cup dry white wine

500 ml / 18 fl. oz / 2 cups fish stock

150 g / 5 oz prepared puff pastry

a little plain (all-purpose) flour, for dusting

1 small egg, beaten

METHOD

1. Heat the olive oil in a large saucepan set
   over a medium heat until hot. Add the leek
   and a little salt and sweat for 4–5 minutes

2. Add the salmon, prawns, mussels and ha
   of the thyme, then add the wine and bring
   a simmer before covering with the stock.

3. Cover with a lid and cook at a simmer for
   3–4 minutes, then spoon the mixture into
   round baking dish. Pick out the mussel m
   from the shells and discard the shells.

4. Preheat the oven to 190°C (170°C fan) / 37
   / gas 5.

5. Roll out the pastry on a lightly floured
   surface into a round approximately 1 cm
   (½ in) thick.

6. Drape over the baking dish and seal again
   the rim of the dish, then cut away the exce

7. Brush with the beaten egg. Bake for
   20–25 minutes until puffed and golden.
   Serve with more thyme as a garnish.

TOP TIP

Rinse the leeks in a couple of changes of water to get rid of any dirt or grit.

addock otato-topped ie

VES **4**

PARATION TIME **25 MINUTES**

KING TIME **1 HOUR 5–10 MINUTES**

GREDIENTS

/ 2 lb 4 oz / 6 ⅔ cups floury potatoes,
eeled and diced

/ 3 ½ oz / ⅓ cup butter

ml / 18 fl. oz / 3 cups whole (full-fat) milk

and freshly ground black pepper

g / 1 lb 5 oz / 4 cups haddock fillet

y leaf

o black peppercorns

w sprigs of tarragon, chopped

METHOD

1. Cook the potatoes in a large saucepan of salted, boiling water for 15–20 minutes until tender to the point of a knife.

2. Drain and leave to cool for a few minutes, then mash with the butter, 4 tbsp of milk and some seasoning. Cover and set to one side.

3. Place the haddock fillet in a large saucepan and cover with the remaining milk, the bay leaf and the peppercorns.

4. Bring to a simmer over a medium heat. Cook at a steady simmer for 4–5 minutes until firm and slightly opaque in appearance.

5. Strain the mixture, discarding the bay leaf and peppercorns but reserving the liquid. Preheat the oven to 180°C (160°C fan) / 350F / gas 4.

6. Spoon the haddock and some of the liquid into the base of a heatproof baking dish. Top with the tarragon and smooth over the mashed potato.

7. Bake the pie for 35–40 minutes until golden on top, then serve.

TOP TIP

Lightly crush the peppercorns to extract as much taste as possible.

Haddock, Cod and Prawn Pie

SERVES 6

PREPARATION TIME 15–20 MINUTES

COOKING TIME 1 HOUR 5–15 MINUTES

INGREDIENTS

1 kg / 2 lb 4 oz / 6 ⅔ cups floury potatoes,
    peeled and diced
110 g / 4 oz / ½ cup unsalted butter
1 tbsp sunflower oil
2 large carrots, peeled and sliced
4 sticks of celery, sliced
1 courgette (zucchini), finely diced
salt and freshly ground black pepper
450 g / 1 lb / 3 cups haddock fillet, cut into chunks
300 g / 10 ½ oz / 2 cups cod fillet, cut into chunks
300 g / 10 ½ oz / 2 cups prawns (shrimp),
    peeled and de-veined
500 ml / 18 fl. oz / 2 cups fish stock
150 g / 5 oz / 1 ½ cups Cheddar, grated

METHOD

1. Cook the potato in a large saucepan of salted, boiling water for 15–20 minutes until tender to the point of a knife.

2. Drain well and leave to cool slightly, then mash with 75 g / 2 ½ oz / ⅓ cup of the butter and some seasoning.

3. Melt the rest of the butter with the oil in a large saucepan. Add the carrot, celery, courgette and a little salt and sweat for 7–8 minutes until softened.

4. Add the fish, prawns and stock. Bring to a simmer and cook uncovered for 5 minutes.

5. Preheat the oven to 180°C (160°C fan) / 3.. / gas 4.

6. Spoon the vegetables, fish and seafood in a large, oval baking dish.

7. Top with the mashed potato and Cheddar and bake for 35–45 minutes until golden brown on top, then serve.

TOP TIP

Let the fish pie stand for 5–10 minutes before serving.

hellfish Pie

GREDIENTS

sp unsalted butter

sp plain (all-purpose) flour, plus extra
for dusting

ml / 1 pint 6 fl. oz / 3 cups whole
full-fat) milk

g / 10 ½ oz / 2 cups prawns (shrimp),
peeled and de-veined

g / 8 oz / 1 ½ cups mussels, cleaned,
with beards removed

g / 10 ½ oz / 2 cups haddock fillet,
cut into chunks

t and freshly ground black pepper

mall bunch of flat-leaf parsley, finely chopped

sp olive oil

g / 10 ½ oz prepared puff pastry

rge egg, beaten

METHOD

1. Melt the butter in a large saucepan set over a medium heat until hot. Add the flour and whisk until you have a smooth roux.

2. Whisk in the milk in a slow, steady stream until smooth and slightly thickened.

3. Bring to a simmer and cook for 2 minutes, then add the prawns, mussels and haddock. Cover with a lid and cook for 3 minutes.

4. Discard any mussels that haven't opened. Pick the meat from the shells and discard the shells.

5. Season the shellfish filling and stir through the parsley. Spoon into 4 individual baking dishes and drizzle with olive oil, then place on a baking tray.

6. Preheat the oven to 180°C (160°C fan) / 350F / gas 4.

7. Roll out the pastry on a lightly floured surface to 1 cm (½ in) thickness and cut out 4 rounds to cover the tops of the dishes.

8. Drape over the dishes and seal well against their rims, cutting away any excess. Brush with the beaten egg and bake for 20–25 minutes until golden and puffed, then serve.

Smoked Trout Pie

SERVES 6

PREPARATION TIME **15 MINUTES**

COOKING TIME **1 HOUR 5–15 MINUTES**

INGREDIENTS

1 kg / 2 lb 4 oz / 6 ⅔ cups floury potatoes,
    peeled and diced
110 g / 4 oz / ½ cup unsalted butter
salt and freshly ground black pepper
2 shallots, finely chopped
150 g / 5 oz / 2 cups chestnut mushrooms,
    finely chopped
750 g / 1 lb 10 oz / 5 cups smoked trout fillet
125 ml / 4 ½ fl. oz / ½ cup dry white wine
250 ml / 9 fl. oz / 1 cup fish stock
75 g / 3 oz / ¾ cup dry breadcrumbs

METHOD

1. Cook the potatoes in a large saucepan of
   salted, boiling water for 15–20 minutes until
   tender to the point of a knife.

2. Drain well and leave to cool for a few
   minutes, then mash with 75 g / 2 ½ oz / ⅓
   cup of butter and some seasoning.

3. Melt the rest of the butter in a large
   saucepan set over a medium heat until hot

4. Add the shallot, mushrooms and a little s
   and sweat for 6–7 minutes until softened.

5. Add the trout and cover with the wine
   and stock. Bring to a simmer and cook
   uncovered for 5 minutes, then season
   to taste.

6. Preheat the oven to 180°C (160°C fan) / 35
   / gas 4.

7. Spoon the trout mixture into the base of a
   oval baking dish and top with the mashed
   potato and breadcrumbs.

8. Bake for 35–40 minutes until golden on to
   then serve.

TOP TIP

Pick through the trout for any bones or cartilage before cooking.

ndividual
ish Pie

RVES 4

EPARATION TIME 30 MINUTES

OKING TIME 1 HOUR 30–40 MINUTES

GREDIENTS

0 g / 1 lb prepared suet pastry

ttle plain (all-purpose) flour, for dusting

0 g / 1 lb 10 oz / 5 cups salmon fillet, diced

0 ml / 5 fl. oz / ⅔ cup dry white wine

ouquet garni

arge eggs

t and freshly ground black pepper

ew chives, finely chopped

arge egg yolks, beaten

METHOD

1. Preheat the oven to 160°C (140°C fan) / 325F / gas 3. Roll out two-thirds of the pastry on a lightly floured surface to ½ cm (¼ in) thickness and use it to line 4 individual pie moulds.

2. Press well into the base and sides, then trim any excess pastry and chill until needed.

3. Place the salmon in a large saucepan and cover with the wine and enough water to submerge, then add the bouquet garni and bring to a simmer over a medium heat.

4. Cook for 6–8 minutes until the fish is firm and cooked, then drain the liquid and discard the bouquet garni.

5. Flake the fish into a bowl. Cook the eggs in a large saucepan of boiling water for 12 minutes.

6. Drain the eggs and refresh in iced water, then peel and chop and add them to the salmon. Season with salt and pepper and stir in the chives.

7. Spoon the mixture into the lined pastries. Roll out the remaining pastry to ½ cm (¼ in) thickness and cut out 4 rounds.

8. Drape over the filling and seal against the side of the lined pastry. Brush the tops with egg yolk and bake for 50–60 minutes until the pastry is cooked through, then serve.

Anchovy Pie

SERVES 6

PREPARATION TIME **10 MINUTES**

COOKING TIME **1 HOUR 10–20 MINUTES**

INGREDIENTS

400 g / 14 oz prepared hot water pastry
a little plain (all-purpose) flour, for dusting
225 g / 8 oz / 1 ½ cups canned anchovy fillets,
    drained
350 g / 12 oz / 3 cups halloumi, sliced
1 lemon, juiced
salt and freshly ground black pepper
1 large egg, beaten

METHOD

1. Preheat the oven to 160°C (140°C fan) / 32
   / gas 3. Roll out two-thirds of the pastry o
   lightly floured surface to 1 cm (½ in)
   thickness and use it to line a 18 cm (7 in)
   springform cake tin.

2. Press well into the base and sides, trimm
   away any excess, then cover and chill.

3. Toss the anchovy fillets with the halloumi,
   lemon juice and seasoning in a mixing bow

4. Arrange the halloumi slices and anchovy
   fillets in the lined pastry. Roll out the
   remaining pastry on a lightly floured
   surface to 1 cm (½ in) thickness.

5. Drape the pastry over the anchovy filling.
   Seal well against the side of the lined past
   then trim the excess.

6. Brush the top with beaten egg and bore a
   small hole in the middle. Bake for 1 hour
   10–20 minutes until the pastry is golden
   and cooked.

7. Remove to a wire rack to cool before turni
   out and serving.

TOP TIP

Take into account the saltiness of the cheese and anchovies when seasoning.

Vegetable Pies

Cheese and Onion Pie

SERVES 4

PREPARATION TIME 20 MINUTES

COOKING TIME 1 HOUR

INGREDIENTS

3 tbsp unsalted butter
2 onions, finely sliced
salt and freshly ground black pepper
150 g / 5 oz / 3 cups baby spinach, washed
150 g / 5 oz / 1 ½ cups Cheddar, grated
3 large eggs, beaten
110 ml / 4 fl. oz / ½ cup whole (full-fat) milk
200 g / 7 oz prepared shortcrust pastry
a little plain (all-purpose) flour, for dusting

METHOD

1. Preheat the oven to 180°C (160°C fan) / 3?
   / gas 4. Melt the butter in a large saucepa
   set over a medium heat until hot.

2. Add the onion and a little salt and sweat
   for 7–8 minutes until softened, then add
   the spinach.

3. Cook for 3–4 minutes until wilted, then
   strain the spinach and onions through
   a colander to extract as much water
   as possible.

4. Roughly chop and move to a large mixing
   bowl. Add the cheese and eggs, stirring we

5. Roll out the pastry on a lightly floured
   surface into a large round approximately
   1 cm (½ in) thick.

6. Drape over a 20 cm (8 in) tart tin, pressing
   well into the base and sides. Cut away any
   excess overhanging pastry and prick the
   base with a fork.

7. Fill with the cheese and onion mixture an
   bake for 35–45 minutes until the pastry is
   golden and cooked.

8. Remove to a wire rack to cool before turn
   out and serving.

TOP TIP

Extract as much water as possible from the spinach before adding to the pie.

umpkin Pie

<KES 4

PARATION TIME 20 MINUTES

KING TIME 45–55 MINUTES

GREDIENTS

g / 1 lb 5 oz / 4 cups pumpkin,
eeled and diced
g / 10 ½ oz / 2 cups floury potatoes,
eeled and diced
g / 3 ½ oz / ½ cup butter
ml / 3 fl. oz / ⅓ cup whole (full-fat) milk
nch of ground nutmeg
and freshly ground black pepper
g / 9 oz prepared puff pastry
tle plain (all-purpose) flour, for dusting
rge egg, beaten

METHOD

1. Cook the pumpkin and potato in a large saucepan of salted, boiling water for 15–20 minutes until tender to the point of a knife.

2. Drain well and leave to cool slightly, then mash with the butter, milk, nutmeg and seasoning. Spoon into the base of 4 individual baking dishes.

3. Preheat the oven to 190°C (170°C fan) / 375F / gas 5.

4. Roll out the pastry on a lightly floured surface into a large round approximately ½ cm (¼ in) thick. Use a sharp knife or large cookie cutter to cut out 4 rounds to top the dishes.

5. Drape the pastry rounds over the dishes and seal against the rims, using a little beaten egg if necessary.

6. Place on a large baking tray and brush their tops with more beaten egg.

7. Bake for 20–25 minutes until the pastry is golden and puffed, then serve.

TOP TIP
Serve these pies fresh from the oven before the pastry lids deflate.

Greek Feta and Spinach Pie

SERVES 6

PREPARATION TIME 20 MINUTES

COOKING TIME 55–60 MINUTES

INGREDIENTS

3 tbsp olive oil
1 onion, finely chopped
1 red onion, finely chopped
½ tsp dried oregano
½ tsp dried thyme
300 g / 10 ½ oz / 6 cups baby spinach, washed
400 g / 14 oz / 2 ½ cups ricotta
200 g / 7 oz / 2 cups feta, crumbled
salt and freshly ground black pepper
4 sheets of filo pastry, kept under a damp towel
3 tbsp unsalted butter, melted

METHOD

1. Preheat the oven to 190°C (170°C fan) / 3 / gas 5 and line the base and sides of a 2 (8 in) springform cake tin with a sheet of greaseproof paper.

2. Heat the oil in a large saucepan set over moderate heat until hot. Sauté the onions 4–5 minutes, stirring frequently, until gol

3. Add the herbs and the spinach and let the spinach wilt over a reduced heat before removing from the heat.

4. Drain the spinach and onions through a colander, then roughly chop and place in a mixing bowl.

5. Add the ricotta and feta; mix well with yo hands and season to taste.

6. Line the prepared tin with 2 sheets of filo pastry, then spoon the filling on top, smoothing with the back of a spoon.

7. Drape the remaining filo sheets on top, tucking the edges over and in, then brush the top with melted butter.

8. Bake for 35–45 minutes until golden on t Remove from the oven and leave to cool a little before turning out and serving.

aprika Pie

VES 4

PARATION TIME **15–20 MINUTES**

KING TIME **50–60 MINUTES**

GREDIENTS

sp sunflower oil

ion, finely sliced

oves of garlic, chopped

and freshly ground black pepper

edium head of cauliflower, cut into florets

g / 8 oz / 1 ½ cups baby potatoes, halved

p smoked paprika

p sweet paprika

g / 12 oz prepared puff pastry

tle plain (all-purpose) flour, for dusting

ge egg yolk, beaten

METHOD

1. Preheat the oven to 180°C (160°C fan) / 350F / gas 4 and heat the oil in a casserole dish set over a medium heat until hot.

2. Add the onion, garlic and a little salt and sweat for 4–5 minutes until softened.

3. Stir in the cauliflower, baby potatoes and paprika, then cover the dish with a lid and cook over a very low heat for 7–8 minutes, stirring occasionally.

4. Roll out two-thirds of the pastry on a lightly floured surface to ½ cm (¼ in) thickness and use to line a round baking dish.

5. Trim away the excess before filling with the cauliflower and potato mixture. Roll out the remaining pastry to the same thickness as before and drape over the baking dish.

6. Seal well against the lined pastry and cut away the excess. Gather and reroll the excess and cut into strips.

7. Brush the top with beaten egg, then decorate with the strips of pastry. Bake for 30–40 minutes until puffed and golden, then serve.

TOP TIP

Grease the baking dish with a little oil before lining with the pastry.

Mushroom and Potato Pie

MAKES **4**

PREPARATION TIME **15 MINUTES**

COOKING TIME **45 MINUTES**

INGREDIENTS

3 tbsp unsalted butter
2 shallots, finely chopped
2 cloves of garlic, minced
salt and freshly ground black pepper
150 g / 5 oz / 2 cups closed cup mushrooms, roughly chopped
150 g / 5 oz / 2 cups chestnut mushrooms, roughly chopped
75 g / 3 oz / 1 cup chanterelles, chopped
450 g / 1 lb / 3 cups floury potatoes, peeled and diced
a small bunch of flat-leaf parsley, chopped
250 g / 9 oz prepared shortcrust pastry
a little plain (all-purpose) flour, for dusting
1 large egg, beaten

METHOD

1. Melt the butter in a large saucepan set over a medium heat until hot. Add the shallot, garlic and a little salt and sweat for 4–5 minutes.

2. Add the mushrooms and potato and continue to cook for 8–10 minutes, stirring occasionally, until softened.

3. Stir through the parsley and adjust the seasoning to taste, then spoon into the base of 4 individual ovenproof mugs.

4. Preheat the oven to 180°C (160°C fan) / 35 / gas 4.

5. Roll out the pastry on a lightly floured surface to 1 cm (½ in) thickness and cut o 4 rounds that will act as lids for the pies.

6. Wet the rims of the mugs with a little wate then drape the pastry lids over them. Sea the lids against the rim using your thumb and forefinger.

7. Score a pattern on top of the pastry with a sharp knife and brush with the beaten egg

8. Arrange on a baking tray and bake for 20–25 minutes until golden brown and cooked before serving.

TOP TIP
The potato and mushrooms will need plenty of seasoning.

Broccoli and Cauliflower Pie

SERVES 4

PREPARATION TIME **15 MINUTES**

COOKING TIME **40–45 MINUTES**

INGREDIENTS

tbsp olive oil

tbsp unsalted butter

medium onions, chopped

medium courgettes (zucchinis), finely diced

medium carrots, peeled and diced

salt and freshly ground black pepper

head of broccoli, prepared into small florets

small head of cauliflower, prepared into small florets

g / 5 oz prepared shortcrust pastry

little plain (all-purpose) flour, for dusting

small egg, beaten

tbsp white sesame seeds

METHOD

1. Preheat the oven to 180°C (160°C fan) / 350F / gas 4. Heat the oil and butter together in a large saucepan set over a medium heat until hot.

2. Sweat the onion, courgette and carrot with a little salt for 5 minutes, stirring occasionally.

3. Add the broccoli and cauliflower and continue to cook over a reduced heat for 3–4 minutes until tender, then spoon into a round pie dish.

4. Roll out the pastry into a 1 cm (½ in) thick round on a lightly floured surface. Drape over the dish, cutting away any excess from the rim.

5. Brush with beaten egg and top with sesame seeds, then bake for 25–30 minutes until golden brown at the edges.

6. Remove from the oven and leave to cool for 5 minutes before serving.

TOP TIP

Use the baking dish as a guide for rolling out the pastry to the correct size.

Cheese and Potato Pie

SERVES 4

PREPARATION TIME 20 MINUTES

COOKING TIME 1 HOUR 10–20 MINUTES

INGREDIENTS

150 ml / 5 fl. oz / ⅔ cup whole (full-fat) milk
150 ml / 5 fl. oz / ⅔ cup double (heavy) cream
2 cloves of garlic, minced
750 g / 1 lb 10 oz / 5 cups floury potatoes,
    peeled and sliced
350 g / 12 oz prepared shortcrust pastry
a little plain (all-purpose) flour, for dusting
150 g / 5 oz / 1 ½ cups reblochon, cubed
150 g / 5 oz / 1 ½ cups Cheddar, grated
salt and freshly ground black pepper
1 large egg, beaten
100 g / 3 ½ oz / 2 cups baby spinach, washed
a few sprigs of dill

METHOD

1. Combine the milk, cream and garlic in a
   saucepan and warm over a medium heat
   until simmering.

2. Add the potato slices and stir well before
   covering with a lid. Cook over a reduced h
   for 5 minutes, then remove from the heat.

3. Preheat the oven to 160°C (140°C fan) / 32
   / gas 3.

4. Roll out two-thirds of the pastry on a light
   floured surface to 1 cm (½ in) thickness ar
   use it to line the base and sides of a 20 cm
   (8 in) square baking dish.

5. Prick the base with a fork, then top with th
   potato and cream mixture. Sprinkle over t
   cheeses and some seasoning, then stir
   briefly to mix.

6. Roll out the remaining pastry into a square
   approximately 1 cm (½ in) thick. Drape ove
   the filling and seal against the edge of the
   other pastry by crimping between thumb
   and forefinger.

7. Brush with beaten egg, then bake for
   45–50 minutes until the pastry is golden
   and cooked. Serve with baby spinach and c
   on the side.

TOP TIP
This pie can be made
in advance and
served cold.

orest
Mushroom Pie

VES 4

PARATION TIME **15 MINUTES**

KING TIME **1 HOUR 10-20 MINUTES**

GREDIENTS

sp unsalted butter

allots, finely chopped

oves of garlic, minced

g / 1 lb / 3 cups mixed wild mushrooms, sliced

mall bunch of flat-leaf parsley, finely chopped

emon, juiced

t and freshly ground black pepper

g / 14 oz prepared hot water pastry

tle plain (all-purpose) flour, for dusting

rge egg, beaten

METHOD

1. Melt the butter in a large saucepan set over a medium heat until hot. Add the shallot, garlic and a little salt and sweat for 5-6 minutes.

2. Add the mushrooms and continue to cook for 5-6 minutes, stirring occasionally.

3. Stir through the parsley and lemon juice and season to taste, then set to one side to cool.

4. Preheat the oven to 160°C (140°C fan) / 325F / gas 3. Roll out two-thirds of the pastry on a lightly floured surface into a large round approximately 1 cm (½ in) thick.

5. Use the pastry round to line the base and sides of a large, round baking dish; let the excess pastry overhang by 5 cm (2 in).

6. Fill with the mushroom mixture. Roll out the remaining pastry into a round the same diameter as the baking dish, approximately 1 cm (½ in) thick.

7. Lay the pastry round on top of the mushrooms, bringing the excess overhanging pastry back over the rim and over the pastry and pleating to seal.

8. Brush with beaten egg and bore a small hole in the middle. Bake for 50-60 minutes until golden and cooked before serving.

Spinach and Goats' Cheese Pie

SERVES 4

PREPARATION TIME 15 MINUTES

COOKING TIME 55–60 MINUTES

INGREDIENTS

3 tbsp olive oil
2 onions, finely chopped
1 tsp dried oregano
½ tsp dried basil
450 g / 1 lb oz / 9 cups baby spinach, washed
300 g / 10 ½ oz / 3 cups goats' cheese, crumbled
salt and freshly ground black pepper
4 large sheets of filo pastry, kept under a
  damp towel
3 tbsp unsalted butter, melted

METHOD

1. Preheat the oven to 180°C (160°C fan) / 3?
   / gas 4.

2. Heat the oil in a large saucepan set over a
   moderate heat until hot, then sweat the
   onions for 5–6 minutes.

3. Add the herbs and the spinach. Let the
   spinach wilt over a reduced heat before
   removing from the heat.

4. Drain the spinach and onions through a
   colander, then roughly chop and place in a
   mixing bowl.

5. Add half of the crumbled goats' cheese and
   mix well, then season to taste.

6. Line an 18 cm (7 in) springform cake tin with
   the sheets of pastry, brushing melted butt
   between each one; let the pastry overhang
   the rim.

7. Spoon the filling on top, smoothing with the
   back of a spoon, then top with the rest of the
   goats' cheese. Bring the overhanging pas
   back over the filling, folding to fit.

8. Bake for 35–40 minutes until cooked
   through. Remove from the oven and leave
   cool a little before turning out and serving

TOP TIP

The pie can be finished under a hot grill to brown the top.

urried
egetable Pie

ERVES 4

REPARATION TIME 15 MINUTES

OOKING TIME 1 HOUR 5–15 MINUTES

INGREDIENTS

- g / 1 lb 5 oz / 4 cups new potatoes
- sp unsalted butter
- ion, finely sliced
- oves of garlic, minced
- and freshly ground black pepper
- low courgette (zucchini), sliced
- o Madras curry powder
- nch of Cayenne pepper
- ml / 9 fl. oz / 1 cup double (heavy) cream
- g / 12 oz prepared puff pastry
- le plain (all-purpose) flour, for dusting
- rge egg, beaten

METHOD

1. Cook the potatoes in a large saucepan of salted, boiling water for 15–20 minutes until tender to the point of a knife.

2. Drain well and leave to cool briefly, then slice. Melt the butter in a large saucepan set over a medium heat until hot.

3. Add the onion, garlic and a little salt. Sweat for 5–6 minutes until softened, then add the courgette. Continue to cook for 2 minutes, then stir in the curry powder and Cayenne.

4. Pour in the cream, bring to a simmer, and cover with a lid. Cook over a low heat for 5 minutes, then season to taste.

5. Preheat the oven to 180°C (160°C fan) / 350F / gas 4. Roll out two-thirds of the pastry on a lightly floured surface into a 1 cm (½ in) thick round.

6. Use the pastry to line a 20 cm (8 in) round baking dish. Cut away any excess overhanging pastry and prick the base with a fork.

7. Fill with the vegetable filling, then roll out the remaining pastry into a 1 cm (½ in) round. Drape over the filling and seal against the other pastry using your thumb and forefinger.

8. Brush with beaten egg and bore a hole in the middle. Bake for 25–30 minutes until golden and puffed, then serve.

Aubergine Pie

SERVES 4–6

PREPARATION TIME 25 MINUTES

COOKING TIME 35–45 MINUTES

INGREDIENTS

350 g / 12 oz prepared puff pastry
a little plain (all-purpose) flour, for dusting
110 ml / 4 fl. oz / ½ cup extra virgin olive oil
1 tsp dried oregano
2 aubergines (eggplants), sliced into thin strips
1 red onion, finely sliced
1 courgette (zucchini), sliced into thin strips
2 cloves of garlic, minced
salt and freshly ground black pepper
1 large egg, beaten
a large handful of rocket (arugula), to serve
2 vine tomatoes, cored and finely diced

METHOD

1. Preheat the oven to 160°C (140°C fan) / 3
   / gas 3. Grease and line a large baking tr
   with a sheet of greaseproof paper.

2. Roll out the pastry on a lightly floured
   surface into a large rectangle approxima
   60 cm x 40 cm (24 in x 16 in) and 1 cm
   (½ in) thick.

3. Cut in half down the middle so that you h
   two identical pieces of pastry. Reserve a
   leftover pastry, reroll to 1 cm (½ in)
   thickness and cut into decorative shapes

4. Lift one piece of the pastry onto the lined
   baking tray. Mix the olive oil with the
   oregano and toss half with the vegetable
   garlic and plenty of seasoning in a
   mixing bowl.

5. Spoon the mixture onto the pastry on the
   baking tray, leaving a 2 cm (1 in) border a
   the way around. Brush the border with se
   beaten egg, then lift the other piece of
   pastry on top of the filling.

6. Seal the pastries together using your
   fingers. Brush the top with more beaten
   then decorate with the pastry shapes and
   brush again with more egg.

7. Bake for 35–45 minutes until golden and
   puffed. Serve with a rocket and tomato sa
   and the remaining olive oil and oregano
   as a dressing.

Savoury Tarts and Pastries

Quiche Lorraine

SERVES 6

PREPARATION TIME 10 MINUTES

COOKING TIME 1 HOUR 10 MINUTES

INGREDIENTS

250 g / 9 oz prepared shortcrust pastry
a little plain (all-purpose) flour, for dusting
2 tbsp unsalted butter
100 g / 3 ½ oz / ⅔ cup pancetta, diced
375 ml / 13 fl. oz / 1 ½ cups whole (full-fat) milk
250 g / 9 oz / 1 cup crème fraiche
5 large eggs
150 g / 5 oz / 1 ½ cups Gruyère, grated
salt and freshly ground black pepper
150 g / 5 oz / 3 cups mixed leaf salad, to serve
75 g / 3 oz / ½ cup cherry tomatoes, halved

METHOD

1. Preheat the oven to 160°C (140°C fan) / 3 / gas 3.

2. Roll out the pastry on a floured surface to 1 cm (½ in) thickness and use it to line a 18 cm (7 in) tart tin. Prick the base with a fork and chill.

3. Melt the butter in a saucepan set over a moderate heat until hot.

4. Add the pancetta and fry for 2–3 minutes until golden, then drain on kitchen paper.

5. Whisk together the milk, crème fraiche, eggs, Gruyère and seasoning until thoroughly incorporated.

6. Arrange the pancetta in the base of the pastry, then pour over the egg filling. Bake for 50–60 minutes until the filling is set and the pastry is cooked.

7. Remove to a wire rack to cool before turning out and serving with salad and cherry tomatoes on the side.

TOP TIP
If the filling is set but slightly wobbly to the touch, it is perfectly cooked.

Cornish Pasty

MAKES 4

PREPARATION TIME 25 MINUTES

COOKING TIME 55–60 MINUTES

INGREDIENTS

2 tbsp unsalted butter

1 large onion, finely chopped

2 small white potatoes, peeled and finely diced

1 turnip, peeled and finely diced

Salt and freshly ground black pepper

450 g / 1 lb / 3 cups steak mince

250 ml / 9 fl. oz / 1 cup beef stock

Few dashes of Worcestershire sauce

350 g / 12 oz prepared shortcrust pastry

A little plain (all-purpose) flour, for dusting

1 large egg, beaten

METHOD

1. Melt the butter in a large casserole dish set over a medium heat until hot. Add the onion, potato, turnip and salt and sweat for 8–10 minutes until softened.

2. Add the steak mince and cook for 4–5 minutes until browned.

3. Cover with the stock and Worcestershire sauce, then stir well and simmer for 8–10 minutes until most of the liquid has evaporated. Season to taste.

4. Preheat the oven to 180°C (160°C fan) / 350F / gas 4.

5. Roll out the pastry on a lightly floured surface to 1 cm (½ in) thickness. Cut out 12 cm (5 in) rounds using a straight-sided cookie cutter.

6. Fill the centre of the rounds with the beef filling, then wet the edges with a little water.

7. Bring the edges of the pastry over the filling to meet above the centre. Seal by crimping between thumb and forefinger and then arrange on a baking tray.

8. Brush the pastries with the beaten egg. Bake for 30 minutes until golden brown and cooked through. Serve either hot or cool.

Spinach and Feta Pastries

MAKES 4

PREPARATION TIME 25 MINUTES

COOKING TIME 20 MINUTES

INGREDIENTS

3 tbsp olive oil
300 g / 10 ½ oz / 6 cups baby spinach, washed
150 g / 5 oz / 1 ½ cups feta cheese, cubed
salt and freshly ground black pepper
250 g / 9 oz prepared shortcrust pastry
a little plain (all-purpose) flour, for dusting
1 large egg, beaten

METHOD

1. Preheat the oven to 190°C (170°C fan) / 375 / gas 5 and line a baking tray with greaseproof paper.

2. Heat the olive oil in a large frying pan set over a moderate heat until hot, then wilt th spinach in the hot oil until soft.

3. Reduce the heat slightly before stirring in the feta. Season to taste, then press the spinach against a colander to extract some water.

4. Roll out the pastry on a lightly floured surface into a large round approximately ½ cm (¼ in) thick. Use a 10 cm (4 in) cookie cutter to cut out rounds of pastry.

5. Place 1 tbsp of the spinach filling in the centre of each round of pastry; wet the rim with a little water.

6. Fold the pastry over the filling to form a semi-circle, making sure to seal the edges well. Arrange on a baking tray and brush th tops with beaten egg.

7. Bake for 14–16 minutes until golden and puffed, then serve.

TOP TIP

For a shinier glaze, beat the egg yolk with 1 tbsp of milk to brush on the pastries.

oats' Cheese nd Leek Tart

VES 4–6

PARATION TIME **15 MINUTES**

KING TIME **1 HOUR 15–20 MINUTES**

GREDIENTS

g / 1 lb 5 oz / 4 cups floury potatoes, peeled
and diced

/ 3 oz / ⅓ cup crème fraiche

and freshly ground black pepper

g / 7 oz / 2 cups goats' cheese, crumbled

sp unsalted butter

rge leek, sliced

g / 9 oz prepared shortcrust pastry

tle plain (all-purpose) flour, for dusting

METHOD

1. Cook the potato in a large saucepan of salted, boiling water for 15–20 minutes until tender to the point of a knife. Drain well and leave to cool slightly.

2. Mash the potato with the crème fraiche and seasoning until smooth, then add the goats' cheese and mash again briefly to incorporate.

3. Preheat the oven to 160°C (140°C fan) / 325F / gas 3.

4. Melt the butter in a large frying pan set over a medium heat until hot. Add the leek and a little salt and sweat for 5–6 minutes until softened, then set to one side.

5. Roll out the pastry on a lightly floured surface into a round approximately 2 cm (1 in) thick. Line a cast-iron pan with the round of pastry, creating a rough border around the rim.

6. Prick the pastry all over with a fork and fill with the potato and cheese filling. Smooth with the back of a spoon, then scatter over half of the sweated leek.

7. Bake for 50–60 minutes until the pastry is cooked through. Serve with the rest of the leek as a garnish on top.

Turkey Pastries

MAKES 8

PREPARATION TIME 25 MINUTES

COOKING TIME 40 MINUTES

INGREDIENTS

2 tbsp unsalted butter
1 tbsp sunflower oil
1 onion, finely chopped
450 g / 1 lb / 3 cups turkey leg meat, diced
150 g / 5 oz / 2 cups fresh breadcrumbs
salt and freshly ground black pepper
400 g / 14 oz prepared puff pastry
a little plain (all-purpose) flour, for dusting
2 large egg yolks, beaten with 1 tbsp water
2 tbsp black sesame seeds

METHOD

1. Preheat the oven to 190°C (170°C fan) / 3 / gas 5. Melt the butter with the oil in a la sauté pan set over a moderate heat until

2. Add the onion and sauté for 3–4 minutes, then add the turkey and cook for 6–7 minutes until browned.

3. Remove the pan from the heat and stir through the breadcrumbs and seasoning to taste.

4. Divide the pastry in half and roll out each piece on a lightly floured surface into lar rectangles that are ½ cm (¼ in) thick.

5. Use a sharp knife to cut out 8 rectangles pastry, 10 cm x 5 cm (4 in x 2 in) in dimens from each piece, giving you 16 rectangles of pastry.

6. Spoon the turkey filling down the middle half of the rectangles, leaving a small border all the way around.

7. Wet the border with some water before lifting the other pastry rectangles on top, seal the pastries together.

8. Arrange on a large baking tray and brush the tops with the egg yolk glaze. Sprinkle over some sesame seeds and bake for 18–22 minutes until golden before servin

Cheese and Tomato Tarts

SERVES 4–6

PREPARATION TIME **10–15 MINUTES**

COOKING TIME **30–35 MINUTES**

INGREDIENTS

300 g / 10 ½ oz prepared shortcrust pastry
little plain (all-purpose) flour, for dusting
large egg yolks
large eggs
250 g / 9 oz / 1 cup crème fraiche
300 g / 10 ½ oz / 3 cups Cheddar, grated
salt and freshly ground black pepper
vine tomatoes, cored and halved
small bunch of sage, leaves picked
small handful of flat-leaf parsley,
 finely chopped
tbsp extra virgin olive oil
tbsp balsamic vinegar

METHOD

1. Preheat the oven to 190°C (170°C fan) / 375F / gas 5.

2. Roll out the pastry on a lightly floured surface into a large rectangle approximately ½ cm (¼ in) thick.

3. Use the pastry to line the base and sides of a shallow rectangular tart tin, then prick the base with a fork and chill.

4. Whisk together the egg yolks, eggs, crème fraiche, Cheddar and seasoning. Spoon over the pastry and top with the tomato halves, cut-side facing up.

5. Sprinkle over the sage and parsley, then drizzle over the olive oil and vinegar.

6. Bake for 30–35 minutes until the pastry is cooked and the filling is set.

7. Remove to a wire rack to cool before turning out and serving.

TOP TIP

This tart can also be browned under a hot grill just before slicing and serving.

131

Pea and Parmesan Pastries

MAKES **4**

PREPARATION TIME **20 MINUTES**

COOKING TIME **35–45 MINUTES**

INGREDIENTS

300 g / 10 ½ oz prepared shortcrust pastry
a little plain (all-purpose) flour, for dusting
150 g / 5 oz / ⅔ cup crème fraiche
150 ml / 5 fl. oz / ⅔ cup whole (full-fat) milk
4 large eggs
150 g / 5 oz / 1 ½ cups Parmesan, grated
110 g / 4 oz / 1 cup peas
4 small tomatoes, cut into wedges
450 g / 1 lb / 3 cups baby carrots, halved
salt and freshly ground black pepper

METHOD

1. Preheat the oven to 180°C (160°C fan) / 35[...] / gas 4.

2. Roll out the pastry on a lightly floured surface to 1 cm (½ in) thickness and cut o[...] 4 rounds of pastry to line the base and sid[...] of 4 tartlet tins.

3. Press the pastry into the base and sides o[...] the tins, then cut away any excess pastry. Prick with a fork.

4. Whisk together the crème fraiche, milk, eggs and Parmesan with a little seasoning[...] Stir through the peas and tomatoes, then spoon the mixture into the pastry cases.

5. Arrange the carrots in patterns on top of t[...] filling, then carefully move the tartlets to [...] baking tray.

6. Bake for 35–45 minutes until the pastry is cooked through and the filling is set.

7. Remove to a wire rack to cool before servin[...]

TOP TIP

Use your thumbs and index fingers to deftly line the cases with the pastry.

Leek, Bacon and Prawn Quiche

SERVES 6

PREPARATION TIME **15 MINUTES**

BAKING TIME **55–60 MINUTES**

INGREDIENTS

300 g / 10 ½ oz / 2 cups prawns (shrimp), peeled

2 tbsp unsalted butter

100 g / 3 ½ oz / ⅔ cup pancetta, diced

1 leek, sliced

4 large sheets of filo pastry

250 g / 9 oz / 1 cup crème fraiche

250 ml / 9 fl. oz / 1 cup double (heavy) cream

4 large eggs

150 g / 5 oz / 1 ½ cups Cheddar, grated

Salt and freshly ground black pepper

1 lemon, thinly sliced

METHOD

1. Preheat the oven to 180°C (160°C fan) / 350F / gas 4. Chop most of the prawns, saving 2 as a garnish.
2. Melt the butter in a large sauté pan set over a medium heat until hot.
3. Add the pancetta and leek and sweat for 6–8 minutes until the leek is soft, then tip into a mixing bowl.
4. Line a 20 cm (8 in) fluted baking dish with the sheets of filo pastry. Add the crème fraiche, cream and eggs to the leek and pancetta.
5. Whisk well before adding the cheese, chopped prawns and seasoning, whisking again briefly to incorporate.
6. Pour into the lined baking dish and top with lemon slices, then bake for 40–45 minutes until the filling is set and the pastry is cooked.
7. Remove to a wire rack to cool before turning out and serving.

TOP TIP

Grease the baking dish with a little oil to prevent the pastry from sticking.

Asparagus and Lemon Tart

SERVES 6

PREPARATION TIME **10 MINUTES**

COOKING TIME **35–40 MINUTES**

INGREDIENTS

250 g / 9 oz / 2 cups asparagus spears,
    woody ends removed
2 lemons
salt and freshly ground black pepper
3 sheets of filo pastry, kept under a damp towel
3 tbsp olive oil
150 g / 5 oz / 1 ½ cups grated mozzarella
55 g / 2 oz / ½ cup pine nuts

METHOD

1. Preheat the oven to 190°C (170°C fan) / 37... / gas 5.

2. Blanch the asparagus in a large saucepa... of salted, boiling water for 2 minutes, the... drain and refresh in iced water.

3. Zest and juice the lemons into a mixing bo... Add the asparagus and toss well before seasoning.

4. Line a 20 cm (8 in) fluted pie dish with the sheets of filo pastry, brushing each with olive oil before lining.

5. Sprinkle over the mozzarella, then top wi... the asparagus and pine nuts.

6. Bake for 25–30 minutes until the pastry is golden before serving.

TOP TIP
You can peel the thicker asparagus spears so that they cook evenly.

Potato and Curry Samosas

MAKES *8*

PREPARATION TIME **25 MINUTES**

COOKING TIME **50-55 MINUTES**

INGREDIENTS

450 g / 1 lb / 5 cups floury potatoes, peeled and finely diced

1 tbsp sunflower oil

1 large onion, finely chopped

2 cloves of garlic, minced

2 green chillies (chilis), deseeded and finely chopped

Salt and freshly ground black pepper

2 tsp Madras curry powder

1 tsp garam masala

350 g / 12 oz prepared shortcrust pastry

A little plain (all-purpose) flour, for dusting

250 g / 9 oz / 1 cup plain yogurt

A small bunch of mint, finely chopped

METHOD

1. Preheat the oven to 180°C (160°C fan) / 350F / gas 4. Cook the potato in a large saucepan of salted, boiling water for 6–8 minutes until tender to the point of a knife.

2. Drain well and leave to cool to one side. Heat the oil in a large saucepan set over a medium heat until hot.

3. Add the onion, garlic, chilli and a little salt. Sweat for 5–6 minutes until softened, then add the spices and stir well.

4. Cook for 1 minute, then add the potato and stir again. Cook over a reduced heat for 2 minutes, then season to taste and set to one side.

5. Roll out the pastry on a lightly floured surface into a large square approximately ½ cm (¼ in) thick and cut out 8 squares approximately 10 x 10 cm (4 x 4 in) in dimension.

6. Spoon the curried potato filling into the centre of the squares. Wet the rims and fold one corner over to the other, crimping to seal.

7. Arrange on a greaseproof paper-lined baking tray and prick with a fork a few times, then bake for 22–25 minutes until golden brown and cooked through.

8. Stir together the yogurt, mint and seasoning to serve with the samosas.

Tomato and Mozzarella Tarts

MAKES **4**

PREPARATION TIME **20 MINUTES**

COOKING TIME **25 MINUTES**

INGREDIENTS

225 g / 8 oz prepared shortcrust pastry
a little plain (all-purpose) flour, for dusting
a large bunch of basil, leaves picked
2 cloves of garlic, chopped
75 g / 3 oz / ¾ cup Parmesan, chopped
110 ml / 4 fl. oz / ½ cup olive oil
salt and freshly ground black pepper
225 g / 8 oz / 1 cup sun-dried tomatoes in oil,
    drained
300 g / 10 ½ oz / 3 cups fresh mozzarella,
    drained and sliced
100 g / 3 ½ oz / ⅔ cup prosciutto slices

METHOD

1. Preheat the oven to 180°C (160°C fan) / 35?
   / gas 4.

2. Roll out the pastry on a lightly floured
   surface to ½ cm (¼ in) thickness. Cut out
   four 15 cm (6 in) rounds and use to line
   4 individual fluted tartlet tins.

3. Prick the bases with a fork and chill.

4. Blend the basil leaves, garlic, Parmesan
   and oil in a food processor, then season
   to taste.

5. Line the pastry cases with overlapping
   circles of sun-dried tomato and mozzarel
   Top with the basil pesto and arrange the t
   on a baking tray and bake the tarts for
   20–25 minutes.

6. Remove to a wire rack to cool, then serve
   with slices of prosciutto.

TOP TIP

Adjust the amount of oil in the pesto for a thicker or thinner sauce as desired.

Pear and Spinach Tart

SERVES 4

PREPARATION TIME 20 MINUTES

COOKING TIME 40–50 MINUTES

INGREDIENTS

250 g / 9 oz prepared shortcrust pastry
Little plain (all-purpose) flour, for dusting
1 tbsp olive oil
150 g / 5 oz / 3 cups baby spinach, washed
Salt and freshly ground black pepper
120 g / 4 oz / 1 cup Cheddar, grated
1 large conference pear, cored and sliced
75 g / 2 oz / ½ cup pine nuts
Pinch of Cayenne pepper

METHOD

1. Preheat the oven to 180°C (160°C fan) / 350F / gas 4.

2. Roll out the pastry on a lightly floured surface into a rectangle approximately 1 cm (½ in) thick.

3. Drape over a fluted rectangular tart tin. Press well into the base and sides and prick the base with a fork, then chill.

4. Heat the olive oil in a large sauté pan set over a medium heat until hot. Add the spinach and some seasoning and cook until wilted.

5. Drain the spinach through a colander and pat dry with kitchen paper, then spread over the base of the pastry.

6. Top with the Cheddar, pear slices and pine nuts, then bake for 25–35 minutes until the pastry is cooked through and golden.

7. Remove to a wire rack to cool before serving with a pinch of Cayenne pepper on top.

TOP TIP

When rolling out the pastry, apply even pressure and roll smoothly.

Ham and Cheese Turnovers

MAKES *8*

PREPARATION TIME *25 MINUTES*

COOKING TIME *30–35 MINUTES*

INGREDIENTS

450 g / 1 lb prepared shortcrust pastry
a little plain (all-purpose) flour, for dusting
8 slices of ham
200 g / 7 oz / 2 cups mozzarella, sliced
2 large eggs, beaten
150 g / 5 oz / 1 cup sesame seeds
150 g / 5 oz / 1 ½ cups golden breadcrumbs

METHOD

1. Preheat the oven to 180°C (160°C fan) / 3
   / gas 4. Roll out the pastry on a lightly
   floured surface into a large round
   approximately 1 cm (½ in) thick.

2. Cut out 8 ovals of pastry approximately
   15 x 10 cm (6 x 4 in) in dimension.

3. Cut the slices of ham to size and arrange
   the pastry ovals, leaving a small border a
   the way around.

4. Top with slices of mozzarella in the centre,
   then brush the borders with some beaten e

5. Fold one edge over the filling and seal
   against the other using your fingers.

6. Brush the sealed turnovers with more
   beaten egg, then dip in a mixture of the
   sesame seeds and breadcrumbs to coat.

7. Arrange on a greaseproof paper-lined
   baking tray and bake for 30–35 minutes
   until cooked through, then serve.

TOP TIP

Don't forget to coat the
undersides of the turnovers
with sesame, as well as
the tops.

Red Onion and Goats' Cheese Tart

SERVES 4–6

PREPARATION TIME 15 MINUTES

COOKING TIME 50–55 MINUTES

INGREDIENTS

- tbsp unsalted butter
- tbsp olive oil
- large red onions, sliced
- clove of garlic, minced
- salt and freshly ground black pepper
- g / 10 ½ oz / 3 cups goats' cheese, crumbled
- g / 9 oz prepared shortcrust pastry
- a little plain (all-purpose) flour, for dusting

METHOD

1. Preheat the oven to 180°C (160°C fan) / 350F / gas 4.

2. Melt the butter with the oil in a frying or sauté pan set over a medium heat until hot.

3. Add the onions, garlic and a little salt and sweat for 10–12 minutes until softened, stirring occasionally.

4. Add the goats' cheese and continue to cook for 2 minutes, then season to taste.

5. Roll out the pastry on a lightly floured surface to 1 cm (½ in) thickness and use it to line a fluted rectangular tart tin.

6. Press into the base and sides and prick the base with a fork, then fill with the onion and cheese mixture.

7. Bake for 30–35 minutes until the pastry is cooked through and golden at the edges, then remove to a wire rack to cool before serving.

TOP TIP

Use a pair of tongs to lift the onions and cheese onto the tart easily.

Salmon and Leek Turnovers

MAKES 4

PREPARATION TIME 20 MINUTES

COOKING TIME 40–45 MINUTES

INGREDIENTS

2 tbsp olive oil
½ large leek, halved, sliced and washed
salt and freshly ground black pepper
450 g / 1 lb / 3 cups skinless salmon fillet, diced
300 g / 10 ½ oz prepared puff pastry
a little plain (all-purpose) flour, for dusting
75 g / 3 oz / ½ cup smoked salmon slices
a small bunch of dill, torn
1 medium egg, beaten
1 lemon, cut into wedges

METHOD

1. Heat the olive oil in a large frying pan set over a medium heat. Add the leek and a li[ttle] salt, then sweat for 4–5 minutes until softened.

2. Add the salmon and cook for 4–5 minutes then season to taste and set to one side.

3. Preheat the oven to 190°C (170°C fan) / 37[5°F] / gas 5 and line a baking tray with greaseproof paper.

4. Roll out the pastry on a lightly floured surface to ½ cm (¼ in) thickness and cut o[ut] 4 rounds approximately 18 cm (7 in) in diameter.

5. Spoon the leek and salmon onto the centr[e] followed by the smoked salmon and some d[ill].

6. Wet the rim of the pastry with a little wate[r] then fold the bottom end over the filling a[nd] seal against the opposite side.

7. Arrange on the baking tray and score a pattern using a sharp knife, then brush wi[th] beaten egg.

8. Bake for 20–25 minutes until the pastry is golden and cooked through. Serve with lemon wedges and more dill.

Crab Quiche

SERVES 6

PREPARATION TIME **15 MINUTES**

COOKING TIME **30–35 MINUTES**

INGREDIENTS

250 g / 9 oz prepared shortcrust pastry
a little plain (all-purpose) flour, for dusting
375 ml / 13 fl. oz / 1 ½ cups whole (full-fat) milk
250 ml / 9 fl. oz / 1 cup double (heavy) cream
3 large eggs
110 g / 4 oz / 1 cup Cheddar, grated
460 g / 1 lb / 3 cups cooked crabmeat
1 small bunch of dill, finely chopped
salt and freshly ground black pepper

METHOD

1. Preheat the oven to 180°C (160°C fan) / 350F / gas 4.

2. Roll out the pastry on a lightly floured surface into a rectangle approximately 1 cm (½ in) thick and use it to line the base and sides of a fluted rectangular tart tin.

3. Prick with a fork and chill as you prepare the filling.

4. Whisk together the milk, cream, eggs and Cheddar in a mixing bowl, then add the crabmeat and dill and season to taste.

5. Pour the filling into the lined pastry case. Bake for 30–35 until the pastry is cooked and the filling is just set.

6. Remove to a wire rack to cool before turning out and serving.

TOP TIP

The quiche can be eaten cold. Cool to room temperature, then cover and chill.

Seafood Empanadas

MAKES 8

PREPARATION TIME 20 MINUTES

COOKING TIME 18–22 MINUTES

INGREDIENTS

400 g / 14 oz / 2 cups canned tuna chunks, drained and flaked
150 g / 5 oz / 1 cup cooked prawns (shrimp), chopped
150 g / 5 oz / 1 ½ cups feta
2 tbsp olive oil
1 lemon, juiced
salt and freshly ground black pepper
350 g / 12 oz prepared puff pastry
a little plain (all-purpose) flour, for dusting
1 large egg, beaten
½ tsp dried oregano
½ tsp dried tarragon
2 tbsp extra virgin olive oil

METHOD

1. Preheat the oven to 190°C (170°C fan) / 350 / gas 5 and line a large baking tray with greaseproof paper.

2. Mix together the tuna, prawns, feta, olive c lemon juice and seasoning in a large mixing bowl.

3. Roll out the pastry on a lightly floured surface into a large round approximately ½ cm (¼ in) thick.

4. Use a cookie cutter to stamp out rounds of pastry approximately 12 cm (5 in) in diamete

5. Spoon the seafood filling onto the centre of the rounds of pastry. Wet the rims with a little water and fold over to seal into empanadas.

6. Lift onto a large baking tray and brush with the beaten egg. Sprinkle over the dried herbs, season and drizzle with extra virgin olive oil.

7. Bake for 18–22 minutes until golden and puffed before serving.

TOP TIP

Twist the cookie cutter to help separate the rounds of dough away from the main pastry.

Sweet Pies

Individual Blueberry Pies

MAKES 6

PREPARATION TIME 1 HOUR

COOKING TIME 25–30 MINUTES

INGREDIENTS

200 g / 7 oz / 1 cup butter, cubed
    and chilled
400 g / 14 oz / 2 ⅔ cups plain
    (all-purpose) flour
400 g / 14 oz / 2 ⅔ cups blueberries
4 tbsp caster (superfine) sugar
½ tsp cornflour (cornstarch)
1 egg, beaten

METHOD

1. Rub the butter into the flour then stir in just enough cold water to make the pastry into pliable dough.

2. Wrap the dough in cling film and chill for 30 minutes.

3. Preheat the oven to 200°C (180°C fan) / 40 / gas 6.

4. Roll out half the pastry on a floured surface and cut out 6 circles to line 6 tartlet tins.

5. Toss the blueberries with the sugar and cornflour and divide between the 6 pastry cases.

6. Roll out the rest of the pastry and cut out 6 circles.

7. Brush the rim of the pastry cases with egg before laying the lids on top then press down firmly round the outside.

8. Cut excess pastry into strips and attach them to the top of the pies in a lattice pattern with a little beaten egg.

9. Brush the top of the pies with more beaten egg then bake in the oven for 25–30 minutes.

10. Transfer the pies to a wire rack to cool.

TOP TIP

Replace the blueberries with blackcurrants and double the amount of caster sugar.

ey Lime Pie

VES 6

PARATION TIME 15 MINUTES

LING TIME 4 HOURS 20 MINUTES

REDIENTS

/ 5 oz / 1 cup digestive biscuits, crushed
/ 3 ½ oz / ½ cup butter, melted
ge egg yolks
/ 2 ½ oz / 1 cup icing (confectioners') sugar
/ 14 oz / 2 cups condensed milk
es, juiced and zested
ped cream, to serve

METHOD

1. Preheat the oven to 180°C (160°C fan) / 350F / gas 4.

2. Combine the crushed biscuits and melted butter in a large mixing bowl until they resemble wet sand.

3. Press the mixture into the base and sides of an 18 cm (7 in) springform tart tin. Bake for 10 minutes, then remove to a wire rack to cool.

4. Beat the egg yolks and icing sugar in a large mixing bowl with an electric whisk, then add the condensed milk and beat thoroughly for 2–3 minutes until thick.

5. Add the lime juice and most of the zest and beat again for 2–3 minutes before pouring into the base. Cover and chill the pie for 4 hours.

6. Turn the pie out after chilling and serve slices with whipped cream and the remaining lime zest to garnish.

TOP TIP

When slicing the pie, warm a sharp knife under hot running water to cut evenly.

Spiced Plum Pie

SERVES 6

PREPARATION TIME 15 MINUTES

COOKING TIME 45–50 MINUTES

INGREDIENTS

300 g / 10 ½ oz prepared shortcrust pastry
a little plain (all-purpose) flour, for dusting
225 g / 8 oz / 1 cup Greek yogurt, whipped
165 g / 5 ½ oz / 1 cup soft dark brown sugar
2 tsp ground cinnamon
1 tsp ground ginger
450 g / 1 lb / 3 cups plums, pitted and cut
    into wedges

METHOD

1. Preheat the oven to 160°C (140°C fan) / 3
   / gas 3.

2. Roll out the pastry on a lightly floured
   surface into a round approximately 1 cm
   (½ in) thick.

3. Use the pastry to line a 20 cm (8 in) flute
   tart tin, pressing well into the base and si

4. Prick with a fork and top with the whippe
   Greek yogurt, then sprinkle over the sug
   and ground spices.

5. Top with the plum wedges and arrange t
   to fit, then bake for 45–50 minutes until
   pastry is cooked through.

6. Remove to a wire rack to cool, then turn
   and serve.

TOP TIP

Mix together the spices in a small pot before sprinkling over the sugar.

akewell Pie

SERVES 6–8

PREPARATION TIME **20 MINUTES**

COOKING TIME **40–45 MINUTES**

INGREDIENTS

0 g / 9 oz prepared shortcrust pastry

g / 2 oz / 1/3 cup plain (all-purpose) flour, plus
extra for dusting

5 g / 8 oz / 1 cup unsalted butter, softened

5 g / 8 oz / 1 cup caster (superfine) sugar

g / 6 oz / 1 3/4 cups ground almonds

arge eggs

sp vanilla extract

olden delicious apples, peeled, cored and
thinly sliced

osp flaked (slivered) almonds

METHOD

1. Preheat the oven to 180°C (160°C fan) / 350F
   / gas 4.

2. Roll out the pastry on a lightly floured
   surface to 1/2 cm (1/4 in) thickness and use it to
   line a 20 cm (8 in) tart tin, pressing well into
   the base and sides.

3. Prick the pastry with a fork and set to
   one side, then beat together the flour,
   butter, sugar, ground almonds, eggs and
   vanilla extract in a large mixing bowl for
   3–4 minutes with an electric whisk until
   thoroughly combined.

4. Spoon the mixture into the pastry case and
   smooth with the back of a tablespoon.

5. Top with a thin layer of apple slices and
   scatter over the flaked almonds.

6. Bake for 40–45 minutes until the pastry and
   filling are cooked and golden.

7. Remove to a wire rack to cool, then serve.

TOP TIP

The butter should be
really soft before
preparing the filling.

Individual Fruit Pies

MAKES 4

PREPARATION TIME 25 MINUTES

COOKING TIME 30–35 MINUTES

INGREDIENTS

350 g / 12 oz prepared shortcrust pastry
a little plain (all-purpose) flour, for dusting
450 g / 1 lb / 3 cups Bramley apples, peeled,
    cored and diced
150 g / 5 oz / 1 cup gooseberries
85 g / 3 ½ oz / ½ cup soft light brown sugar
2 large egg whites
110 g / 4 oz / ½ cup caster (superfine) sugar
½ tsp cream of tartar
150 g / 5 oz / 1 cup redcurrants
1 tbsp icing (confectioners') sugar, for dusting

METHOD

1. Preheat the oven to 180°C (160°C fan) / 35 / gas 4. Roll out the pastry on a lightly floured surface to ½ cm (¼ in) thickness and cut out four rounds of pastry to line individual tartlet tins.

2. Drape the pastry over the tins and press well into the base and sides, cutting away any excess.

3. Line with greaseproof paper and fill with baking beans, then blind-bake for 12–15 minutes until golden at the edges.

4. Remove to a wire rack to cool and discard the baking beans and greaseproof paper.

5. Combine the apple, gooseberries, brown sugar and 2 tbsp of water in a saucepan, then cook over a low heat until the fruit is soft and mushy.

6. Beat the egg whites in a large, clean mixing bowl until they form soft peaks. Add half the caster sugar and beat until thick and shiny.

7. Add the cream of tartar and the remaining sugar and continue to beat until glossy, then spoon into a piping bag fitted with a star nozzle. Increase the oven to 220°C (220°C fan) / 425F / gas 7.

8. Spoon the fruit compote into the pastry and pipe over swirls of meringue, then surround with redcurrants and bake for 15–18 minutes until the meringue is golden brown.

9. Remove to a wire rack and leave to cool slightly, then dust with icing sugar to serve.

anana and hocolate Pie

RVES 4

EPARATION TIME 15 MINUTES

OKING TIME 25 MINUTES

GREDIENTS

) g / 7 oz prepared shortcrust pastry
ttle plain (all-purpose) flour, for dusting
nall egg, beaten
) g / 9 oz / 1 cup chocolate and hazelnut spread
rge bananas, sliced
ipped cream, to serve
g / 2 oz / 1/3 cup dark chocolate

METHOD

1. Preheat the oven to 190°C (170°C fan) / 375F / gas 5.

2. Roll out the pastry on a lightly floured surface to ½ cm (¼ in) thickness and use it to line an 18 cm (7 in) straight-sided tart tin.

3. Press the pastry into the base and sides before cutting away any excess.

4. Prick the base with a fork and line with greaseproof paper, then fill with baking beans and blind bake for 12–15 minutes until golden brown.

5. Remove from the oven and discard the beans and the greaseproof paper. Brush the base with the beaten egg and return to the oven for 4 minutes.

6. Remove to a wire rack to cool slightly, then spread the chocolate and hazelnut spread over the base and top with slices of banana.

7. Return to the oven for 2–3 minutes to glaze. Remove and leave to cool slightly, then turn out and serve with whipped cream and dark chocolate grated over.

TOP TIP

Warm the chocolate and hazelnut spread in a microwave to make it easier to spread.

Blueberry Pie

SERVES 6–8

PREPARATION TIME **10 MINUTES**

COOKING TIME **30–35 MINUTES**

INGREDIENTS

250 g / 9 oz prepared shortcrust pastry
a little plain (all-purpose) flour, for dusting
1 small egg, beaten
350 g / 12 oz / 1 ½ cups fromage blanc
350 g / 12 oz / 1 ½ cups vanilla yogurt
1 tbsp lemon juice
½ tsp vanilla extract
runny honey, to drizzle
300 g / 10 ½ oz / 2 cups blueberries

METHOD

1. Preheat the oven to 180°C (160°C fan) / 35
   / gas 4. Roll out the pastry on a lightly
   floured surface into a round approximatel
   ½ cm (¼ in) thick and use it to line the base
   and sides of a 20 cm (8 in) fluted tart tin.

2. Trim any excess pastry and discard, then
   prick the base all over with a fork.

3. Line the pastry with greaseproof paper
   and fill with baking beans before blind
   baking for 15–18 minutes until the edges
   are golden brown.

4. Remove from the oven and discard the
   greaseproof paper and baking beans.

5. Return the pastry to the oven for
   4–5 minutes to brown the base.

6. Remove again and brush with the beaten
   egg, then return to the oven for another
   2 minutes. Remove to a wire rack to cool.

7. Beat together the fromage blanc, yogurt,
   lemon juice and vanilla extract in a large
   mixing bowl until smooth.

8. Carefully remove the pastry from the tin a
   filling with the fromage blanc filling. Drizz
   with some runny honey, then top with mos
   of the blueberries and serve the remainde
   on the side.

ustard Cream
ie

RVES 88

EPARATION TIME 15 MINUTES

)KING TIME 1 HOUR 20–25 MINUTES

GREDIENTS

g / 9 oz prepared shortcrust pastry

ttle plain (all-purpose) flour, for dusting

ml / 12 fl. oz / 1 ½ cups double (heavy) cream

ml / 9 fl. oz / 1 cup whole (full-fat) milk

sp vanilla extract

rge eggs

g / 5 oz / ⅔ cup caster (superfine) sugar

METHOD

1. Preheat the oven to 180°C (160°C fan) / 350F / gas 4. Roll out the pastry on a lightly floured surface to 1 cm (½ in) thickness and use it to line a 20 cm (8 in) tart tin.

2. Press well into the base and sides, cut away any excess pastry and prick the base with a fork.

3. Line the pastry with greaseproof paper and fill with baking beans, then blind bake for 15 minutes. Remove to a wire rack and discard the greaseproof paper and beans.

4. Return to the oven for 5 minutes before removing again and setting to one side.

5. Reduce the oven temperature to 150°C (130°C fan) / 300F / gas 2 and combine the cream, milk and vanilla extract in a saucepan.

6. Bring the cream mixture to the boil, then remove from the heat. Beat together the eggs and sugar in a heatproof bowl until thick and frothy.

7. Whisk with the cream mixture until incorporated and smooth, then strain into a jug.

8. Pour into the pastry case and bake for 50–60 minutes until set. Remove to a wire rack to cool before serving.

Cherry Pie

MAKES **4**

PREPARATION TIME **30 MINUTES**

COOKING TIME **40 MINUTES**

INGREDIENTS

300 g / 10 ½ oz prepared shortcrust pastry
a little plain (all-purpose) flour, for dusting
400 g / 14 oz / 2 cups canned morello cherries,
    drained
2 tbsp whole (full-fat) milk
1 tbsp caster (superfine) sugar

METHOD

1. Roll out two-thirds of the pastry on a light
   floured surface to approximately 1 cm (½
   thickness and cut out four rounds to line t
   base and sides of the moulds of a
   cupcake tin.

2. Line four moulds with the pastry and trim
   any excess pastry, then prick the bases ar
   chill for 15 minutes.

3. Preheat the oven to 180°C (160°C fan) / 35
   / gas 4. Roll out the remaining pastry to th
   same thickness as before and cut out
   rounds of pastry approximately 5 cm
   (2 in) thick.

4. Prick the pastry lids a few times with a for
   then remove the pastry from the fridge an
   fill with the cherries.

5. Wet the rims of the lined pastry with a littl
   water. Place the pastry lids on top and crir
   the edges together to seal.

6. Bake the pies for 30–35 minutes until the
   pastry is cooked and lightly golden, then
   whisk together the milk and sugar until th
   sugar has dissolved.

7. Remove the pies from the oven and brush
   the tops with the glaze. Return to the oven
   for a few minutes to brown the glaze
   before serving.

emon
Meringue Pie

VES 6-8

PARATION TIME 25 MINUTES

KING TIME 45 MINUTES

GREDIENTS

g / 9 oz prepared shortcrust pastry
tle plain (all-purpose) flour, for dusting
g / 1 lb / 2 cups lemon curd
sp cornflour (cornstarch)
edium egg yolks
edium egg
edium egg whites, at room temperature
ch of salt
g / 5 oz / ⅔ cup caster (superfine) sugar
cream of tartar

METHOD

1. Preheat the oven to 190°C (170°C fan) / 375F / gas 5. Roll out the pastry on a floured surface to ½ cm (¼ in) thickness and use it to line an 18 cm (7 in) springform cake tin.

2. Prick the pastry with a fork, then line with cling film and fill with baking beans. Blind bake for 15 minutes.

3. Beat the lemon curd with 1 tbsp of water and half the cornflour in a saucepan, then cook over a low heat, stirring constantly, for 3–4 minutes.

4. Beat in the egg yolks and whole egg until thickened, then remove from the heat and leave to cool.

5. Whisk the egg whites and salt in a clean bowl until they form soft peaks. Add half the sugar and beat until stiff.

6. Add the remaining sugar, cornflour and cream of tartar, continuing to beat until glossy.

7. Fill the pastry with the curd mixture and spread the meringue on top in mounds.

8. Bake for 20–25 minutes until golden on top, then remove from the oven and leave to cool before serving.

Fig Pie

SERVES 6

PREPARATION TIME 35 MINUTES

COOKING TIME 50–55 MINUTES

INGREDIENTS

225 g / 8 oz prepared shortcrust pastry
a little plain (all-purpose) flour, for dusting
2 large eggs
75 g / 3 oz / ⅓ cup caster (superfine) sugar
100 g / 3 ½ oz / ⅔ cup self-raising flour
150 ml / 5 fl. oz / ⅔ cup whole (full-fat) milk
½ tsp vanilla extract
2 tbsp unsalted butter, melted
450 g / 1 lb / 3 cups ripe figs, halved
a few sprigs of thyme, to garnish

METHOD

1. Preheat the oven to 160°C (140°C fan) / 3 / gas 3.

2. Roll out the pastry on a lightly floured surface to ½ cm (¼ in) thickness and use line a 20 cm (8 in) pie dish, pressing well the base and sides.

3. Trim any excess pastry and chill the past case for 20 minutes.

4. Beat together the eggs and sugar in a mi: bowl until thick and frothy, then fold in the flour.

5. Whisk in the milk, vanilla extract and melted butter in that order until you have smooth batter.

6. Pour the batter into the pastry case and arrange the fig halves on top.

7. Bake for 50–55 minutes until the pastry i golden and the batter is set. Remove from the oven and garnish with thyme before serving.

TOP TIP

Use dried figs sliced in half for a sweeter taste and chewy texture.

Apple and Cherry Pie

SERVES 6–8

PREPARATION TIME **15–20 MINUTES**

COOKING TIME **1 HOUR 15–20 MINUTES**

INGREDIENTS

350 g / 12 oz prepared shortcrust pastry
a little plain (all-purpose) flour, for dusting
225 g / 8 oz / 2 cups ground almonds
110 g / 4 oz / ½ cup caster (superfine) sugar
150 g / 5 oz / ⅔ cup unsalted butter
3 small eggs
3 small egg whites
3 eating apples, peeled, cored and sliced
350 g / 12 oz / 2 ⅓ cups cherries, pitted
2 large egg yolks, beaten

METHOD

1. Preheat the oven to 160°C (140°C fan) / 325F / gas 3. Roll out two-thirds of the pastry on a lightly floured surface to 1 cm (½ in) thickness.

2. Line the base and sides of a 20 cm (8 in) pie dish with the pastry. Trim away the excess and prick the base with a fork, then chill.

3. Pulse together the almonds, sugar, butter, eggs and egg whites in a food processor until smooth, then scrape into a mixing bowl.

4. Add the apple slices and cherries and stir well to combine, then spoon into the lined pastry.

5. Roll out the remaining pastry on a lightly floured surface to the same thickness as before, then drape over the filling and crimp against the lined pastry.

6. Trim the excess pastry and brush the top with the beaten egg before scoring indents around the rim of the pastry.

7. Bake for 1 hour until the pastry is golden and cooked through; the filling should be set.

8. Remove to a wire rack to cool slightly before serving.

Raspberry Cream Pie

SERVES **4**

PREPARATION TIME **15 MINUTES**

COOKING TIME **20 MINUTES**

INGREDIENTS

250 g / 9 oz prepared shortcrust pastry
a little plain (all-purpose) flour, for dusting
1 small egg, beaten
450 g / 1 lb / 2 cups mascarpone
65 g / 2 ½ oz / ½ cup icing (confectioners') sugar,
    plus extra for dusting
1 lemon, juiced
125 g / 4 ½ oz / 1 cup raspberries

METHOD

1. Preheat the oven to 180°C (160°C fan) / 350°F / gas 4.

2. Roll out the pastry on a lightly floured surface to 1 cm (½ in) thickness and use it to line a 15 cm (6 in) fluted pie dish, pressing well into the base and sides.

3. Cut away any excess pastry and prick the base with a fork.

4. Line with greaseproof paper and fill with baking beans, then blind bake for 15 minutes.

5. Remove from the oven and discard the beans and paper, then return to the oven for 2 minutes before removing again.

6. Brush the base with the beaten egg and return to the oven for 2 minutes, then remove to a wire rack to cool.

7. Beat together the mascarpone, icing sugar and lemon juice until smooth, then spoon into the cooled pastry case and top with raspberries.

8. Dust with icing sugar before serving.

TOP TIP

Use a large balloon whisk to beat the mascarpone; this will give a lighter texture.

Pear Pie

SERVES 6–8

PREPARATION TIME 20 MINUTES

COOKING TIME 35–40 MINUTES

INGREDIENTS

350 g / 12 oz prepared puff pastry
little plain (all-purpose) flour, for dusting
100 g / 4 oz / 1 cup ground almonds
100 g / 4 oz / ½ cup unsalted butter, softened
100 g / 3 ½ oz / ½ cup caster (superfine) sugar
1 small egg
1 small egg white
800 g / 1 lb 12 oz / 4 cups canned pear halves
  in juice, drained
2 large egg yolks

METHOD

1. Preheat the oven to 180°C (160°C fan) / 350F
   / gas 4. Roll out two-thirds of the pastry on a
   lightly floured surface into a rectangle
   approximately ½ cm (¼ in) thick.

2. Line the base and sides of a rectangular
   baking dish with the pastry. Prick the base
   with a fork and trim as necessary on
   the sides.

3. Pulse together the almonds, butter, sugar,
   egg and egg white in a food processor until
   creamy, then spread out evenly across the
   base of the pastry.

4. Top with the pear halves, then roll out
   the remaining pastry into a rectangle
   approximately ½ cm (¼ in) thick. Drape
   over the filling and seal against the sides
   of the pastry.

5. Brush the top with the beaten egg yolk and
   bake for 35–40 minutes until golden brown
   all over.

6. Remove from the oven and leave to stand
   briefly before serving.

TOP TIP

Reserve some of the
pear juice from the
cans and serve it
with the pie.

Rhubarb Crumble

SERVES 6

PREPARATION TIME **10–15 MINUTES**

COOKING TIME **1 HOUR 10–15 MINUTES**

INGREDIENTS

600 g / 1 lb 5 oz / 4 cups rhubarb,
    trimmed and diced
175 g / 6 oz / 1 ½ cups raspberries
1 tsp vanilla extract
a pinch of salt
225 g / 8 oz / 1 cup caster (superfine) sugar
150 g / 5 oz / 1 cup plain (all-purpose) flour,
    plus extra for dusting
150 g / 5 oz / ⅔ cup unsalted butter,
    cold and cubed
300 g / 10 ½ oz prepared shortcrust pastry

METHOD

1. Preheat the oven to 180°C (160°C fan) / 350°F / gas 4. Place the rhubarb, raspberries, vanilla extract and salt in a saucepan with half of the sugar and 2 tbsp of water.

2. Cover and cook over a low heat, stirring occasionally until softened, then set to one side.

3. Line a large rectangular baking dish with a sheet of greaseproof paper. Pulse the flour with the remaining sugar and butter in a food processor until the mixture resembles breadcrumbs.

4. Roll out the pastry on a lightly floured surface to approximately 1 cm (½ in) thickness and use it to line the base and sides of the baking dish.

5. Prick the base with a fork, then sprinkle over a quarter of the crumble mixture. Top with the fruit and the rest of the crumble mixture.

6. Bake for 50–60 minutes until the pastry and crumble are golden and cooked, then serve immediately.

TOP TIP

Discard any rhubarb leaves during preparation, as these can be toxic.

ummer Fruit ie

SERVES 6–8

PREPARATION TIME 25 MINUTES

BAKING TIME 25 MINUTES

INGREDIENTS

g / 9 oz prepared shortcrust pastry
le plain (all-purpose) flour, for dusting
eet of gelatine
mon, juiced
g / 14 oz / 2 cups cream cheese
g / 6 oz / ¾ cup golden caster (superfine) sugar
g / 10 oz / 1 ¼ cups Greek yogurt
o vanilla extract
g / 5 oz / 1 cup strawberries, hulled and halved
g / 4 oz / 1 cup blackberries
g / 4 oz / 1 cup raspberries
g / 4 oz / 1 cup blueberries
all bunch of mint, leaves picked

METHOD

1. Preheat the oven to 180°C (160°C fan) / 350F / gas 4. Roll out the pastry on a lightly floured surface to 1 cm (½ in) thickness and use it to line a 20 cm (8 in) fluted tart tin.

2. Press the pastry well into the base and sides before removing any excess.

3. Prick the pastry with a fork and line with greaseproof paper and baking beans. Blind bake for 15 minutes, then remove from the oven.

4. Discard the beans and paper and return the pastry to the oven for 4–5 minutes until the base browns, then remove to a wire rack to cool.

5. Meanwhile, soften the gelatine in the lemon juice and 1 tbsp of cold water for 5 minutes.

6. Heat the mixture in a small saucepan over a low heat until the gelatine has dissolved.

7. Beat together the cream cheese and the sugar in a large mixing bowl using an electric hand-held whisk for 2 minutes, then add the Greek yogurt and the gelatine mixture and mix again until smooth.

8. Add the vanilla extract and beat well before pouring into the pastry case.

9. Cover and chill for 4 hours until set. Garnish the rim with the fruit and mint leaves before serving.

Orange Meringue Pie

SERVES 8

PREPARATION TIME 55 MINUTES

COOKING TIME 25–30 MINUTES

INGREDIENTS

2 tsp cornflour (cornstarch)
2 oranges, juiced and zest finely grated
2 lemons, juiced and zest finely grated
4 large eggs, beaten
225 g / 8 oz / 1 cup butter
175 g / 6 oz / ¾ cup caster (superfine) sugar

For the pastry:
100 g / 3 ½ oz / ½ cup butter, cubed
200 g / 7 oz / 1 ⅓ cups plain (all-purpose) flour

For the meringue:
4 large egg whites
100 g / 3 ½ oz / ½ cup caster (superfine) sugar

METHOD

1. Preheat the oven to 200°C (180°C fan) / 3
   / gas 6.

2. Rub butter into the flour and add cold wa
   to bind.

3. Chill for 30 minutes then roll out on a
   floured surface.

4. Use the pastry to line a 24 cm loose-
   bottomed tart tin and prick it with a fork.

5. Line the pastry with clingfilm and fill
   with baking beans or rice, then bake for
   10 minutes.

6. Remove the clingfilm and beans and coo
   for 8 minutes.

7. Dissolve the cornflour in the orange and
   lemon juice and put it in a pan with the re
   of the ingredients.

8. Stir constantly over a medium heat to me
   the butter and dissolve the sugar. Pour it
   into the pastry case.

9. Whisk the egg whites until stiff, then
   gradually add the sugar and whisk until t
   mixture is thick and shiny.

10. Spoon the meringue on top of the orange
    mixture, leaving a border round the edge
    and make peaks. Bake for 10 minutes.

TOP TIP

Add 1 tsp of ground cinnamon to the filling before pouring it into the pastry case.

Sweet Tarts and Pastries

Chocolate Tart

SERVES *6–8*

PREPARATION TIME *20 MINUTES*

COOKING TIME *25 MINUTES*

INGREDIENTS

250 g / 9 oz prepared shortcrust pastry
a little plain (all-purpose) flour, for dusting
1 large egg, beaten
300 g / 10 ½ oz / 2 cups good-quality dark
    chocolate, chopped
250 ml / 9 fl. oz / 1 cup double (heavy) cream
1 tbsp liquid glucose
2 tbsp unsalted butter

METHOD

1. Preheat the oven to 190°C (170°C fan) / 37
   / gas 5. Roll out the pastry on a lightly
   floured surface to 1 cm (½ in) thickness
   and use to line a 20 cm (8 in) tart tin.

2. Prick the base with a fork and line with
   greaseproof paper and baking beans.

3. Blind-bake for 12–15 minutes until golden
   then remove and discard the baking beans
   and paper.

4. Brush with beaten egg and return to the
   oven for 5 minutes. Remove and leave to
   cool on a wire rack.

5. Melt the chocolate, cream and liquid gluce
   in saucepan set over a medium heat, stirr
   until smooth.

6. Remove from the heat, then beat in the
   butter and leave to cool for 5 minutes.

7. Pour the chocolate filling into the pastry
   and chill for at least 2 hours before servin

TOP TIP

Sprinkle the tart with chopped mixed nuts before serving to add texture.

pple Tart

SERVES 6

PREPARATION TIME **10–15 MINUTES**

COOKING TIME **25–30 MINUTES**

INGREDIENTS

g / 7 oz prepared shortcrust pastry

ttle plain (all-purpose) flour, for dusting

olden delicious apples, peeled, cored and thinly sliced

mon, juiced

g / 4 oz / ½ cup caster (superfine) sugar

sp unsalted butter, cold and cubed

METHOD

1. Preheat the oven to 190°C (170°C fan) / 350F / gas 5.

2. Roll out the pastry on a lightly floured surface to 1 cm (½ in) thickness. Invert a 20 cm (8 in) diameter plate onto the pastry and cut around it with a sharp knife.

3. Line a baking tray with a sheet of greaseproof paper, then carefully lift the pastry round onto the paper.

4. Prick with a fork, then toss the slices of apple with the lemon juice and sugar in a large mixing bowl.

5. Overlap the slices on top of the pastry to cover it. Spoon over any juice and sugar in the bowl and dot with the butter.

6. Bake for 25–30 minutes until the pastry is cooked through before serving.

TOP TIP

If slicing the apples ahead of time, dress with lemon juice to prevent browning.

Treacle Tart

SERVES 6–8

PREPARATION TIME 10–15 MINUTES

COOKING TIME 50–55 MINUTES

INGREDIENTS

250 g / 9 oz prepared shortcrust pastry
a little plain (all-purpose) flour
300 g / 10 ½ oz / 1 cup golden syrup, warmed
150 g / 5 oz / ½ cup treacle, warmed
225 g / 8 oz / 3 cups breadcrumbs
110 g / 4 oz / ½ cup clotted cream, to serve

METHOD

1. Preheat the oven to 180°C (160°C fan) / 35
   / gas 4.

2. Roll out the pastry on a lightly floured
   surface to 1 cm (½ in) thickness and use i
   line a 20 cm (8 in) springform tart tin.

3. Press the pastry well into the base and si
   before cutting away any excess.

4. Prick the base with a fork, then line with
   greaseproof paper and baking beans.
   Blind bake for 15 minutes, then remove
   from the oven.

5. Discard the beans and paper, then mix
   together the golden syrup, treacle and
   breadcrumbs in a mixing bowl and spoon
   into the pastry case.

6. Bake for 35–40 minutes until set, then
   remove from the oven and leave to cool o
   a wire rack.

7. Slice and serve with clotted cream on
   the side.

TOP TIP

Using stale bread for your breadcrumbs will produce the best results.

Cinnamon Pastry

MAKES 8

PREPARATION TIME **10 MINUTES**

COOKING TIME **15–20 MINUTES**

INGREDIENTS

250 g / 9 oz prepared puff pastry
little plain (all-purpose) flour, for dusting
150 g / 5 oz / ²/₃ cup caster (superfine) sugar
2 tbsp ground cinnamon
50 g / 2 oz / ¼ cup unsalted butter, melted

METHOD

1. Preheat the oven to 190°C (170°C fan) / 375F / gas 5 and line a large baking tray with a sheet of greaseproof paper.

2. Roll out the puff pastry on a lightly floured surface into a large rectangle approximately 1 cm (½ in) thick.

3. Sprinkle over the sugar and cinnamon, spreading it out evenly over the pastry.

4. Roll the rectangle into a sausage shape and brush with melted butter. Cut into 8 pieces and arrange, cut-side down, on the baking tray.

5. Brush all over with more melted butter and bake for 15–20 minutes until puffed and golden.

6. Remove to a wire rack to cool before serving.

TOP TIP

Chilled puff pastry is easier to work with than pastry that is room temperature.

Strawberry Freeform Tart

SERVES 6–8

PREPARATION TIME 20 MINUTES

COOKING TIME 20–25 MINUTES

INGREDIENTS

250 g / 9 oz prepared shortcrust pastry
a little plain (all-purpose) flour, for dusting
1 small egg, beaten
375 ml / 13 fl. oz / 1 ½ cups double (heavy) cream
1 tsp vanilla extract
100 g / 3 ½ oz / ¾ cup icing (confectioners') sugar,
    for dusting
300 g / 10 ½ oz / 2 cups strawberries,
    hulled and halved

METHOD

1. Preheat the oven to 180°C (160°C fan) / 350(
   / gas 4. Roll out the pastry on a lightly
   floured surface into a round approximately
   1 cm (½ in) thick and use it to line a 20 cm
   (8 in) fluted tart tin.

2. Press well into the base and sides of the ti
   trimming any excess pastry.

3. Prick the base with a fork, then line with a
   sheet of greaseproof paper and fill with
   baking beans.

4. Blind bake for 12–15 minutes until golden a
   the edges, then remove from the oven and
   discard the beans and paper.

5. Return the pastry to the oven to brown for
   3–4 minutes, then remove again and brush
   the base and sides with the beaten egg.

6. Return to the oven for 2 minutes, then
   remove to a wire rack to cool as you prepar
   the filling.

7. Whip the cream with the vanilla extract an
   most of the icing sugar in a mixing bowl un
   softly peaked.

8. Remove the pastry from the tin and fill with
   the whipped cream. Top with strawberries
   and a dusting of icing sugar before serving

Chocolate Eclairs

MAKES 12

PREPARATION TIME 25 MINUTES

COOKING TIME 45–50 MINUTES

INGREDIENTS

250 g / 9 oz prepared choux pastry
375 ml / 13 fl. oz / 1 ½ cups whole (full-fat) milk
1 vanilla pod, split lengthwise
4 medium egg yolks
55 g / 2 oz / ¼ cup caster (superfine) sugar
1 tbsp plain (all-purpose) flour
1 ½ tbsp cornflour (cornstarch)
250 ml / 9 fl. oz / 1 cup double (heavy) cream
300 g / 10 ½ oz / 2 cups dark chocolate, chopped
1 tbsp golden syrup

METHOD

1. Preheat the oven to 160°C (140°C fan) / 325F / gas 3 and line a large baking tray with a sheet of greaseproof paper.

2. Spoon the choux pastry into a piping bag fitted with a large, straight-sided nozzle. Pipe 15 cm (6 in) fingers of pastry onto the prepared baking tray, spaced apart.

3. Bake for 30–35 minutes until golden brown and slightly puffed, then remove to a wire rack to cool.

4. Combine the milk and vanilla pod in a saucepan. Bring to a simmer over a medium heat before removing to one side.

5. Whisk together the egg yolks and sugar in a heatproof bowl until pale and thick, then sift in the flour and cornflour and whisk again briefly.

6. Whisk over the warm milk in a slow, steady stream before pouring into a clean saucepan. Cook over a low heat for 2–3 minutes, stirring constantly, until thickened.

7. Transfer the cream filling to a clean bowl, then cover and chill until cold.

8. Once cold, spoon the filling into a piping bag fitted with a nozzle; bore a hole through the centre of the choux pastries and pipe the filling into them.

9. Bring the cream to the boil in a saucepan. Pour over the chocolate and golden syrup in a bowl and leave for a minute before whisking until smooth.

10. Leave to cool and thicken before spreading over the eclairs and serving.

Apricot and Almond Tart

SERVES 6–8

PREPARATION TIME 20 MINUTES

COOKING TIME 50–55 MINUTES

INGREDIENTS

275 g / 10 oz prepared shortcrust pastry
a little plain (all-purpose) flour, for dusting
225 g / 8 oz / 2 cups ground almonds
110 g / 4 oz / ½ cup caster (superfine) sugar
150 g / 5 oz / ⅔ cup unsalted butter
2 medium eggs
2 medium egg whites
350 g / 12 oz / 1 ¾ cups apricot jam (jelly)
3 tbsp flaked (slivered) almonds

METHOD

1. Preheat the oven to 180°C (160°C fan) / 350F / gas 4. Roll out the pastry on a lightly floured surface to 1 cm (½ in) thickness and use it to line a 20 cm (8 in) tart tin.

2. Press well into the base and sides before trimming any excess, overhanging pastry. Prick the base with a fork and chill.

3. Prepare the filling by blitzing together the ground almonds, sugar and butter in a food processor until creamy. Add the eggs and egg whites and pulse well until combined.

4. Fill the pastry case with the filling before topping with the apricot jam.

5. Bake for 45–50 minutes until the pastry and filling are cooked. Top with the flaked almonds and return to the oven for 5 minutes.

6. Remove to a wire rack to cool before turning out and serving.

TOP TIP

Warming the apricot jam before spreading it over the filling will make the task easier.

Egg Custard Tarts

AKES 8

REPARATION TIME 20 MINUTES

OOKING TIME 25 MINUTES

INGREDIENTS

0 g / 10 ½ oz prepared puff pastry

little plain (all-purpose) flour, for dusting

50 ml / 12 fl. oz / 1 ½ cups whole (full-fat) milk

cm (1 in) stick of cinnamon

tsp vanilla extract

25 g / 8 oz / 1 cup caster (superfine) sugar

medium egg yolks, beaten

tbsp cornflour (cornstarch)

tbsp icing (confectioners') sugar

tsp ground cinnamon

METHOD

1. Preheat the oven to 190°C (170°C fan) / 375F / gas 5. Roll out the pastry on a lightly floured surface to ½ cm (¼ in) thickness.

2. Cut out 8 rounds and use them to line 8 individual fluted tartlet tins. Trim any excess overhanging pastry, then chill.

3. Combine the milk, cinnamon stick and vanilla extract in a saucepan. Bring to a simmer over a moderate heat, then set to one side.

4. Beat together the sugar and egg yolks in a heatproof bowl until pale and thick. Sift over the cornflour and beat again to incorporate.

5. Pour a little of the hot milk over the egg yolk mixture, whisking well, then whisk in the remaining milk.

6. Pour the mixture back into a clean saucepan and cook for 2–3 minutes over a low heat, stirring constantly, until thickened.

7. Discard the cinnamon stick and let the custard cool a little before pouring into the pastry cases. Bake for 14–16 minutes until the pastry is golden and cooked.

8. Remove to a wire rack to cool, then turn out and dust with icing sugar and ground cinnamon.

Orange Tart

SERVES 4

PREPARATION TIME 20 MINUTES

COOKING TIME 35–40 MINUTES

INGREDIENTS

150 g / 5 oz prepared shortcrust pastry
a little plain (all-purpose) flour, for dusting
2 large oranges
110 g / 4 oz / ½ cup unsalted butter, softened
100 g / 3 ½ oz / 1 cup ground almonds
100 g / 3 ½ oz / ½ cup caster (superfine) sugar
1 medium egg
½ tsp vanilla extract

METHOD

1. Preheat the oven to 170°C (150°C fan) / 325 / gas 3. Roll out the pastry on a lightly floured surface to ½ cm (¼ in) thickness.

2. Use it to line an 18 cm (7 in) straight-sided tart tin. Prick the base and trim any excess overhanging pastry.

3. Slice one of the oranges and set to one side as a garnish; zest and juice the other into a mixing bowl.

4. Add the softened butter, ground almonds, sugar, egg and vanilla extract and beat well until smooth and creamy.

5. Spread the mixture evenly over the base of the pastry with a palette knife.

6. Bake for 30–35 minutes until the pastry is cooked through and the filling is set, then preheat the grill to hot.

7. Flash the tart under the hot grill to brown the top. Remove to a wire rack to cool befor turning out.

8. Slice and serve with the reserved orange slices.

TOP TIP

If you have a chef's blowtorch, you can use it to brown the top of the tart.

Tarte au Citron

SERVES 6–8

PREPARATION TIME 20 MINUTES

COOKING TIME 1 HOUR

INGREDIENTS

- 250 g / 9 oz prepared shortcrust pastry
- a little plain (all-purpose) flour, for dusting
- 4 medium eggs
- 225 g / 8 oz / 1 cup golden caster (superfine) sugar
- 2 lemons, juiced and zested
- 125 ml / 4 ½ fl. oz / ½ cup double (heavy) cream

METHOD

1. Preheat the oven to 180°C (160°C fan) / 350F / gas 4. Roll out the pastry on a lightly floured surface into a round approximately ½ cm (¼ in) thick.

2. Use the pastry round to line a 20 cm (8 in) fluted tart tin. Press well into the base and sides, trimming any excess overhanging pastry.

3. Prick the base with a fork and line with greaseproof paper before filling with baking beans. Blind-bake for 12–15 minutes until golden at the edges.

4. Remove from the oven and discard the beans and paper, then return the pastry to the oven for 4–5 minutes.

5. Remove again. Beat one of the eggs and use to brush the base and sides of the pastry, then return to the oven for 2 minutes.

6. Remove to a wire rack to cool and reduce the oven to 160°C (140°C fan) / 324F / gas 3.

7. Beat the remaining eggs with the sugar, lemon juice and zest in a large mixing bowl until the sugar has dissolved.

8. Stir in the cream, then strain into a jug and pour into the pastry case. Bake for 30–35 minutes until just set.

9. Remove to a wire rack to cool before turning out and serving.

Pear and Chocolate Tart

SERVES 6

PREPARATION TIME 10–15 MINUTES

COOKING TIME 30–35 MINUTES

INGREDIENTS

225 g / 8 oz prepared puff pastry
a little plain (all-purpose) flour, for dusting
250 g / 9 oz / 1 cup chocolate and hazelnut spread
2 large conference pears, peeled, cored and sliced
1 digestive biscuit, crushed

METHOD

1. Preheat the oven to 190°C (170°C fan) / 375F / gas 5. Line a 20 cm (8 in) round baking tray with a sheet of greaseproof paper.

2. Roll out the pastry on a lightly floured surface into a 22 cm (9 in) round approximately 1 cm (½ in) thick.

3. Lift onto the baking tray and prick the base with a fork.

4. Spread the chocolate and hazelnut spread evenly over the pastry, leaving a 2 cm (1 in) border all the way around.

5. Top with the pear slices and arrange them to fit as necessary, then fold the 2 cm (1 in) border back over the pear slices to make a rim.

6. Bake for 20–25 minutes until the pastry is golden and cooked through.

7. Remove to a wire rack to cool, then garnish with the crushed biscuit and serve.

TOP TIP
Use a warmed palette knife to spread the chocolate and hazelnut spread.

Raspberry Tarts

MAKES 8

PREPARATION TIME 20 MINUTES

COOKING TIME 20 MINUTES

INGREDIENTS

300 g / 10 ½ oz prepared shortcrust pastry
A little plain (all-purpose) flour, for dusting
300 g / 10 ½ oz / 2 ½ cups raspberries
50 g / 2 oz / ½ cup shelled pistachios, finely sliced
1 bsp pumpkin seeds, crushed
1 bsp icing (confectioners') sugar

METHOD

1. Preheat the oven to 180°C (160°C fan) / 350F / gas 4.

2. Roll out the pastry on a lightly floured surface to ½ cm (¼ in) thickness. Cut out 8 ovals of pastry and use them to line 8 individual oval fluted tartlet tins.

3. Prick the bases with a fork and line with greaseproof paper, then fill with baking beans and blind bake for 12–14 minutes until golden brown.

4. Remove from the oven and discard the beans and paper, then return to the oven for 3–4 minutes to brown the bases.

5. Remove to a wire rack to cool.

6. Once cool, fill with the raspberries, arranging them to fit neatly in each tart.

7. Top with the sliced pistachios and crushed pumpkin seeds. Dust lightly with icing sugar before serving.

TOP TIP

A tea strainer is good for dusting individual pastries and tarts with icing sugar.

Chocolate and Hazelnut Tart

SERVES *6*

PREPARATION TIME *20 MINUTES*

COOKING TIME *25 MINUTES*

INGREDIENTS

225 g / 8 oz prepared shortcrust pastry
a little plain (all-purpose) flour, for dusting
350 ml / 12 fl. oz / 1 ½ cups double (heavy) cream
1 tbsp liquid glucose
300 g / 10 ½ oz / 2 cups dark chocolate, chopped
225 g / 8 oz / 2 cups hazelnuts (cobnuts)

METHOD

1. Preheat the oven to 180°C (160°C fan) / 350 / gas 4. Roll out the pastry on a lightly floured surface into a round approximately ½ cm (¼ in) thick.

2. Use the round of pastry to line an 18 cm (7 i tart tin. Press well into the base and sides before trimming any excess, overhanging pastry.

3. Prick the base with a fork and line with greaseproof paper, then fill with baking beans and blind-bake for 12–15 minutes until golden at the edges.

4. Remove from the oven and discard the beans and paper, then return to the oven fo 4–5 minutes to brown the base.

5. Remove to a wire rack to cool.

6. Combine the cream and liquid glucose in a saucepan. Bring to the boil before removin to one side.

7. Pour over the chocolate in a heatproof bowl and leave for 1 minute, then whisk until smooth.

8. Leave to cool and thicken slightly.

9. Arrange the hazelnuts in the base of the pastry before topping with the chocolate filling. Leave to set before serving.

Apple Strudel

SERVES 6–8

PREPARATION TIME 15 MINUTES

COOKING TIME 30–40 MINUTES

INGREDIENTS

350 g / 12 oz prepared puff pastry

little plain (all-purpose) flour, for dusting

750 g / 1 lb 10 oz / 5 cups eating apples, peeled, cored and diced

100 g / 3 ½ oz / ⅔ cup raisins

100 g / 4 oz / ½ cup caster (superfine) sugar

sp ground cinnamon

tsp ground nutmeg

lemon, juiced

large egg, beaten

bsp flaked (slivered) almonds

bsp icing (confectioners') sugar, for dusting

METHOD

1. Preheat the oven to 190°C (170°C fan) / 375F / gas 5 and grease and line a large baking tray with greaseproof paper.

2. Roll out the pastry on a lightly floured surface into a 30 x 20 cm (12 x 8 in) rectangle approximately ½ cm (¼ in) thick.

3. Toss together the apples, raisins, sugar, ground spices and lemon juice in a large mixing bowl.

4. Spoon the filing evenly down one side of the pastry so that it is offset from the centre. Leave a 2 cm (1 in) border on the side of the pastry with the filling.

5. Brush the whole border with beaten egg and fold the pastry over the filling to meet the other border, sealing well.

6. Carefully lift onto the baking tray and brush the top with beaten egg. Sprinkle over the flaked almonds.

7. Bake for 30–40 minutes until the pastry is golden and cooked through. Remove to a wire rack to cool.

8. Dust with icing sugar before slicing and serving.

INDEX

Salmon and Prawn Pie, 80
Smoked Salmon and Herb Pie, 76
Smoked Trout Fish Pie, 88

YOGURT
Blueberry Pie, 168
Potato and Curry Samosas, 139
Spiced Plum Pie, 160
Summer Fruit Pie, 187